MANAGING YOUR MONEY

A practical guide

Michael Wilson

Inter-Varsity Press

INTER-VARSITY PRESS
38 De Montfort Street, Leicester LE1 7GP, England

First published 1994

British Library Cataloguing in Publication Data
A catalogue record for this book is available from the British Library.
ISBN 0–85111–222–6

Phototypeset in Great Britain by Intype, London
Printed in Great Britain by Cox & Wyman Ltd, Reading

Inter-Varsity Press is the book-publishing division of the Universities and Colleges Christian Fellowship (formerly the Inter-Varsity Fellowship), a student movement linking Christian Unions in universities and colleges throughout the United Kingdom and the Republic of Ireland, and a member movement of the International Fellowship of Evangelical Students. For information about local and national activities write to UCCF, 38 De Montfort Street, Leicester LE1 7GP.

CONTENTS

PREFACE

Whether we have it or we don't, we simply can't ignore the power which money exerts on our lives. I believe it is important for Christians to look at what the Bible teaches about money – and the earlier in life we do this, the better.

We all learn through experience, and I've certainly been through a few financial scrapes myself. In fact, I was thinking of dedicating this book 'to my bank manager, to whom I owe so much', but thought better of it in case he decided to make life even more difficult than it is already.

So this book is not written from a lofty, unpractical viewpoint, but is based on real experience. It has been written by someone who knows what it's like to feel under financial pressure.

The final chapter is all about tax and estate planning, about which I know remarkably little. So I would like to thank my good friend Gordon Pickering for having contributed this chapter.

One golden rule for you to remember, even if you take nothing else away from this book: if you are not coping with your finances, *seek help*. To every financial problem there is an answer, but bottling up difficulties will just make things worse. So pray about any problems you have, then discuss them with someone. After all, this person may be the very one God has sent in answer to your prayer.

Michael Wilson

WHAT'S IT ALL ABOUT?

1

Money. The root of all evil? Or a necessary element of western civilization? What should the Christian's attitude be towards money? Are we right to strive to accumulate as much as we can, or are we better off with as little of it as possible? Is money meant to be saved or spent? How much money should a Christian have? Is it right for Christians to borrow money? Should we give all our money away?

*L*iving in the world

If you find yourself asking questions about your own attitude to money, you are probably

"Better the little that the righteous have than the wealth of many wicked"
(Psalm 37:16)

on the right track. The danger for Christians is that it is all too easy to inherit attitudes from the world around us without giving full and proper thought to our own response as Christians.

This book recognizes that it is just about impossible for a Christian to survive without money. You may well write to tell me all about your Christian commune which lives off the labour of the fit and healthy and barters with the outside world, and it would indeed be interesting to learn more about such experiences. But this book is intended for those in the mainstream of the world and for those who have no alternative but to deal with money issues just about every day.

"Man heaps up wealth, not knowing who will get it"
(Psalm 39:6)

Please do not allow yourself to feel too disillusioned if you get the feeling you are not managing your finances well. This book does not set out to illustrate your failures, but aims to provide some practical hints and sources of advice, while attempting to place the whole subject within a Christian context.

I hope this book will be particularly useful for couples about to be married, or newly married. If attitudes to the management of money can be agreed early on in married life, or even earlier, then this will act as a very useful foundation for the future.

It is just as important, however, for single people to address this subject. It may be that, because a single person finds he or she is not accountable to anyone for the management of domestic finances, the result could be an ill-considered or even selfish approach to the subject. We all need God's wisdom.

Have a look at 1 Corinthians 1:18–25. Paul explains that this world's wisdom is foolishness, and what seems to be God's foolishness is, in fact, wiser than human wisdom. So do not be perturbed if you find yourself out of step with those around you.

Money is often the source of serious conflict, whether the problem be on an international scale (such as a war over oil rights) or whether it concerns a local domestic dispute (such as a quarrel between husband and wife). It is no bad thing to pause and think about the whole subject of money and finance, even if we have no natural interest in the subject. Some time spent in thought, prayer and Bible study will do much to lay firm foundations. Paul's words to Timothy promise great things:

Command those who are rich in this present world not to be arrogant nor to put their hope in wealth, which is so uncertain, but to put their hope in God, who richly provides us with everything for our enjoyment. Command them to do good, to be rich in good deeds, and to be generous and willing to share. In this way they will lay up treasure for themselves as a firm foundation for the coming age, so that they may take hold of the life that is truly life.

(1 Timothy 6:17–19)

In today's world, it is often the wealthy who gain respect from others in society. While the Bible does not condemn wealth in itself, it does contain many warnings about wealth's dangers.

Now, think back to the beginning of this chapter. Hands up those who allowed themselves just a little bit of pride in realizing that the Bible doesn't say *money* is the root of all evil, but the *love* of money. Good. Allow yourself two points. The verse you were thinking

"Why should I fear . . . those who trust in their wealth?"
(Psalm 49:5–6, 16–20)

"Though your riches increase, do not set your heart on them"
(Psalm 62:10)

7

of is 1 Timothy 6:10. This passage, which starts at verse 3, encourages us to have an attitude of contentment rather than getting involved in fruitless arguing. A spirit of contentment will make us feel grateful for what we have and will stop us being over-ambitious to gain worldly riches.

People who want to get rich fall into temptation and a trap and into many foolish and harmful desires that plunge men into ruin and destruction. For the love of money is a root of all kinds of evil. Some people, eager for money, have wandered from the faith and pierced themselves with many griefs.

(1 Timothy 6:9–10)

The Bible is a real help in pointing out many of the danger signals relating to our attitude to money. Have a look through the passages from the Psalms and Proverbs scattered through the margins of this chapter.

Security

The first chapter of James reminds us that all we have has come from God, and our personal circumstances can change without warning: 'Every good and perfect gift is from above, coming down from the Father of the heavenly lights, who does not change like shifting shadows.' Although we have to be prepared to accept changes in our lives, whether for better or for worse, we can be assured in the knowledge that our God does not change.

(James 1:17)

"Lazy hands make a man poor . . ."
(Proverbs 10:4, 16)

It would be easy to assume that money in the bank equals happiness and protection from life's trials. This is not so. Certainly, a healthy bank balance does solve some of life's day-to-day problems, but a Christian knows that his or her life is going to contain all sorts of trials. James tells us to expect testing – but we are also told that such times make us 'mature and complete'. So there would be no point in Christians attempting to use money as a form of protection from life's troubles; we shall probably face various trials despite our money, and if we don't, we are losing out on an opportunity to be made pure and complete!

(James 1:4)

Our God-given conscience and God-formed common sense should help us to establish a satisfactory attitude towards money. But, as with most Christian dilemmas, it is important to remember to keep Christ at the centre of what we do, and to put the needs of others before our own – and that is easier said than done.

". . . whoever trusts in his riches will fall"
(Proverbs 11:4, 28)

Full consideration of our Christian responsibility towards giving will go a long way to help resolve many of the issues surrounding money. We shall look at giving in chapter 4.

*P*lanning the future

Once you have come to some conclusions about the part that money plays in your life, you can use the same conclusions to help make decisions about other important areas, such as career development. This should help you answer questions such as:

- Do I think this is the sort of job God wants me to do?

"A sinner's wealth is wealth is stored up for the righteous"
(Proverbs 13:22)

"The poor are shunned . . ., but the rich have many friends"
(Proverbs 14:20)

- Should I always select the job which pays the best salary?
- Is this job consistent with the gifts which God has given me?

A Christian develops a self-worth which does not have to rely on the usual worldly ideals of wealth and status. Have you ever met someone who is totally motivated and driven by the status and responsibility of his or her job? It sometimes seems that the job has taken over the person completely. It is different for the Christian, because career is no longer at the centre – Christ is. A Christian has no need for the comfort and security of a high-profile and impressive job. That is not to say that God will not appoint some Christians to extremely influential positions; but for the individual concerned, it is not the job which is the driving force, but the wish to be a follower of Christ.

This is why it is important that you use the gifts God has given you. If your gifts are not being used in your job, it will not be long before you find yourself being motivated by money rather than a wish to fulfil the job itself – and that will bring its own dissatisfaction.

God has provided each one of us with different gifts and talents which equip us for a variety of jobs and responsibilities. It could well be that, by using the gifts you have received, you earn a good living. You should not be afraid of earning money, neither should you allow such fear to prevent a proper use of your gifts. If you are blessed with a high income, it is not necessarily yours to keep and enjoy anyway. You have to think about how you are going to use your earnings.

"He who loves pleasure will become poor"
(Proverbs 21:17)

Similarly, thinking and praying about the gifts you have received from God will help you to decide what tasks you could consider taking on within the local church – and perhaps even highlight some existing jobs you do for which you have no apparent gift! As Christians, we have to think carefully about our use of all our gifts and talents, and forming a God-centred attitude to money is part of this same process.

a balanced view

" . . . the borrower is servant to the lender"
(Proverbs 22:1, 4, 7)

Balance. That's what we need when thinking about money. Look at those around you and weigh their approach to money on an imaginary scale. Are they heavy on extravagance but light on genuine generosity? Are they economical in the extreme, but storing up treasures for themselves?

Come back to yourself, though. It can be useful to learn from your observation of others, but don't let that get in the way of examining yourself in the same critical light. It is not our place to judge others, but we do have to apply Christ's way to ourselves.

You could say that the 'traditional Christian approach' to money tells you to spend the least possible in any set of circumstances. This is not necessarily Christ's way.

For example, James paints a rather colourful, but unpleasant, picture of wealth.

Now listen, you rich people, weep and wail because of the misery that is coming upon you. Your wealth has rotted, and moths have eaten your clothes. Your gold and silver are corroded. Their corrosion

(James 5:1–3)

will testify against you and eat your flesh like fire. You have hoarded wealth in the last days.

You may well feel that you hardly fit the description 'wealthy', but when you consider the poverty experienced by most people in the world today, you are probably wealthy without really realizing it. Here, in James's letter, the criticism is not about wealth itself, but about its misuse. The accusation is that 'You have hoarded wealth in the last days' instead of using the assets for some good.

(James 5:4)

James goes on to say, 'Look! The wages you failed to pay the workmen who mowed your fields are crying out against you.' If you are ever given the responsibility of employing others, here you have clear evidence that Christians are expected to be fair, and even generous. It is not extravagance if you are helping to contribute to someone else's domestic budget! This applies whether you are employing a whole workforce, or paying someone to do your gardening.

Furthermore, I dare to suggest that this principle extends to the employment of those engaged in Christian work. If we support a pastor, do we expect him or her to live off a lower salary than we enjoy ourselves?

Christians can so easily acquire a reputation for being tight-fisted. We soon justify a parsimonious attitude by saying, 'But it's the Lord's money.' Of course it is, but I believe the Bible's teaching clearly tells us to develop a generous attitude – to others, that is, and not to ourselves! If we genuinely put the needs of others before our own, we can't possibly be accused of being tight-fisted. Let people see an open palm instead of a clenched fist.

"Do not wear yourself out to get rich . . ."
(Proverbs 23:4–5)

THE AGONY COLUMN

Have a go at working out your own answers before you read mine.

Q **I don't believe Jesus wants me to live a shabby, second-rate existence, so why should't I use my money to improve my standard of living?**

A *This is a major dilemma. If you look around, you will see a variety of lifestyles and a variety of attitudes towards money and wealth. Do not let this variety lead you to conclude that your own attitude towards money is unimportant; on the contrary, it is vital you search your heart and apply God's Word to your own life and circumstances. You will probably find it easier to decide what other people ought to be doing with their money than to resolve the issue for yourself.*

It is difficult to answer your question without knowing more of your personal circumstances. It is just not possible to make sensible decisions about money and our standard of living without taking into account other aspects of life.

Let me try to put the question in context. Assume the question was put by a medical missionary working in Africa, who feels it is right to settle there and live in the community in which he serves. Apart from the need for medical supplies and other materials required for the job, money is not likely to be much of an issue. It is not expected that the missionary will feel led to buy a Rolls Royce for himself.

"Better a poor man whose walk is blameless . . ."
(Proverbs 28:6, 22)

Had the question been posed by a Christian businessman whom God is using to good effect in the business community, however, we could not necessarily condemn him for running a Rolls Royce. That doesn't necessarily make it right either, but it can be seen by these two examples that context can make all the difference. Part of the answer to the question must take into account thought for those around us.

What does need to be resolved is the basic attitude to money, and whose money it is anyway. This is where you need to be put on the spot, because the question refers to the use of 'my money'. If we keep in mind that there is nothing in this life that we Christians can call truly our own, and that everything we hold has been provided by God, then perhaps we shall become less possessive about possessions.

"Give me only my daily bread"
(Proverbs 30:7–9)

Q I am considering going to work for a missionary organization. Although this will be a full-time post, I have to give an undertaking that I will raise most of my support myself. I am concerned about making provision for the future, and wonder what I should do about saving up for my pension.

A Some missionary societies pay salaries, in which case they usually make a contribution into a pension scheme. So you should enquire further about this particular society, as it may be that although you have to generate your own support, the money is paid back as salary.

If there is no pension arrangement, you are

right to be concerned, especially if you plan to work for the society for a number of years. Although there are some organizations which exist to relieve the poverty of retired missionaries, it would be better if you were able to allow for an element of savings within your budget, so that you could put something to one side for pension provision. You would need to take advice on this, and the missionary society should be able to point you in the right direction.

WALKING THE TIGHTROPE

Income and expenditure

2

C H A P T E R

*"Is work
simply a way
of obtaining the
money we need
for daily
survival?"*

**One of life's permanent respons-
ibilities seems to be making sure our
expenditure does not exceed our
income. We don't always manage to
achieve it! But before we look at
ways of balancing the books, let's
investigate the way we receive our
income.**

Most of us have to work for our living at
some time or other. So what is work, and why
exactly do we work? Is it simply a way of
obtaining the money we need for daily survival, or is there more to it?

The main aspect of work which frequently
crops up in the Bible relates to the need to
work for six days, but rest on the seventh. 'Six

days you shall labour, but on the seventh day you shall rest; even during the ploughing season and harvest you must rest.'

(Exodus 34:21)

This verse is usually quoted – quite rightly – as an encouragement to rest one day a week. It also encourages us, however, to work the other six! Indeed, this is part of why we were created: God placed Adam in the Garden of Eden 'to work it and take care of it'.

(Genesis 2:15)

Work became a struggle at the fall. God said to Adam:

Cursed is the ground because of you;
through painful toil you will eat of it
all the days of your life.
It will produce thorns and thistles for you,
and you will eat the plants of the field.
By the sweat of your brow
you will eat your food . . .

(Genesis 3:17–19)

So the answer to the question 'Why do we work?' must be that God created us to work – just as he, himself, works – even though our sinful nature means that 'painful toil' is now a feature of our working lives. Moreover, without work we are unlikely to be able to feed ourselves!

We probably won't have a choice as to whether we need to work or not, so what sort of work ought we to be doing?

As a Christian, you may feel the choice is between 'full-time Christian work' and secular work. If you feel called by God to work full time in Christian service, the organization you join might pay you a salary, or it might ask you to raise all or part of your own support from other Christians. This is a rather specialized aspect of personal finance, and I would

> " 'Painful toil' is now a feature of our working lives"

expect anyone who does decide to go 'full time' to obtain proper advice and counselling on the subject.

Of course, Christians who are in secular employment are still full-time Christians! They must be. Christians in work can do a lot with their time and money to further God's work.

*M*atching income to expenditure

Many people monitor their personal finances simply by looking at their bank statement each month. This gives a general impression of how things are going, but is unlikely to provide a proper system of control. Furthermore, management by bank statement can be very misleading, because there will be numerous peaks and troughs in expenditure throughout the year. It would be much better to draw up for yourself a plan of income and expenditure along the following lines.

"Management by bank statement can be very misleading"

WHERE THE MONEY GOES

	Weekly	Monthly
Housing		
Mortgage/rent		
Council tax		
Water rates		
Property repairs, decorating, *etc.*		
Gas		
Electricity		
Other fuel		
Other housing expenditure		

Domestic expenditure
  Food and drink
  Toiletries/cosmetics
  Telephone/postage
  Television: rental/
    licence
  Newspapers, magazines
    and books
  Confectionery and
    children's pocket
    money
  Cleaning materials
  Other

Insurance
  Life and pension
    premiums
  Mortgage endowment
    premiums
  Buildings and contents
    premiums
  Car insurance
  Other

Travel
  Car tax
  Repairs
  Petrol
  Road rescue
    subscriptions
  Fares/season ticket
  Other travel costs

Credit
  Car loan
  Credit cards
  Budget schemes
  Other loans

Other expenditure
  Clothing
  Furniture/carpets
  Recreation/leisure
    activities
  Holidays
  Work costs (*e.g.* tools,
    special clothing)
  Gifts to church/mission-
    ary societies/
    charities/
    individuals
  Miscellaneous

TOTAL EXPENDITURE

INCOME (after all deduc-
  tions for tax, *etc.*)

Less expenditure

Surplus for savings

It is not always possible to predict precise figures, and some bills come at irregular intervals. You should decide whether it is going to be more helpful to work out your budget on a weekly or on a monthly basis. If you prefer weekly, divide quarterly figures by 13 and six-monthly figures by 26 to arrive at an average weekly amount. You'll then need to set the money aside (and resolve not to touch it!) until each bill arrives.

Whichever way you draw up your personal budget, the amount you spend will never work out exactly as you have planned, but at least this will be a start to understanding where your money goes. Take into account any likely fluctuation in income, perhaps because of a change in your pattern of overtime, or the receipt of bonuses.

Although plans change, the exercise is well worth doing, even as just a 'one-off' to help you see how well you are doing.

Of course, when you come to the end of the 'Where the Money Goes' table, you may find you have a deficit instead of a surplus. But by detailing all your expenditure, it should be possible to identify where savings can be made.

*W*hy be so boringly organized?

I have to realize that this whole business of getting organized with budgets and the paying of bills is not everyone's idea of excitement. Let's face it, it's dull and boring.

Actually, it's a bit more than that. It's downright frightening. Now be honest: as you have been reading this chapter, have you been filled with enthusiasm to get down to some serious budgetary control?

There are some people who do actually enjoy getting to grips with their finances and they can readily appreciate the need to keep in control. Others, however, will be just a little frightened of getting organized. It may be that you would much rather bury your head in the sand and wait for the bank statement to arrive to find out how well you are doing. But that is back to management by bank statement, and that simply will not do.

With some preparation and planning, you can put yourself firmly in the driving seat, rather than feeling that it is your bank man-

" . . . not everyone's idea of excitement"

ager who controls your money. He doesn't – but you must.

So why is it you may be afraid of your own finances?

Let me indulge in a little analysis. You probably feel guilty that you are not spending your money as wisely as you should, and you are aware that you are not immune to the occasional bout of impulse buying – after all, we are all bombarded by advertising, and it is only human to give in once in a while. At the same time, you quite like to feel you have the freedom to spend your money as you like. There is probably an unexpressed feeling that if you made yourself a slave to a rigid budget, you would lose some of this freedom, and some of life's enjoyment would dissipate. After all, you work hard, so why shouldn't you spoil yourself occasionally?

The only way I can suggest you overcome this mental block is to make up your mind what your rules are going to be – something like this:

"Why shouldn't you spoil yourself occasionally?"

- I am the one who is in control, not the bank manager.
- I will make sure that I enjoy planning and controlling my finances. I will inject some fun into the proceedings.
- I will recognize my weaknesses, but allow for them in the monthly budget. If I know I am likely to buy clothes once a month, then I shall include a reasonable amount for this in the 'Where the Money Goes' table.
- I will realize at the outset that, no matter how well I plan my budget, unforeseen circumstances will arise. I must expect the unexpected, and not be too downhearted

when things don't work out in accordance with the plan. Life isn't that easy.

- If possible, I shall try to keep a small balance in my current account to act as a buffer for the unexpected.

You will probably recognize that if you are going to set about doing a proper planning job, you are going to be forced into change. Nobody likes change very much; in fact, most people are frightened of change to some extent. That is probably the root problem. You may not want to examine your finances too carefully in case this makes you face the truth, and are forced to change something.

Once you realize how unhelpful this attitude is, you may be more inclined to put good theory into practice.

a regular routine

Assuming you have completed the 'Where the Money Goes' table, you will now have an idea of your total weekly or monthly expenditure. But the trouble is, not all expenditure comes in handy, regular amounts.

The most helpful thing will be to iron out as many of the peaks and troughs as possible by converting many of your commitments to monthly payments. This will apply to regular items such as

- gas
- electricity
- telephone
- local taxes (council tax and water)
- insurance

"Iron out as many of the peaks and troughs as possible"

"... no longer receiving red reminders and threats to be cut off"

Not only will this make the monthly routine so much easier – you simply let the bank pay the amount due by direct debit or standing order – but it is amazing how much pressure will be removed, simply because you are no longer receiving red reminders and threats to be cut off.

Monthly budget accounts for gas, electricity and telephone work out as follows. We shall use gas as an example.

The gas company will examine your gas usage by reference to your gas bills over the previous year or so. They will then estimate your usage over the next twelve months, and this will give rise to a total cost for the year. This figure will simply be divided by twelve to produce the monthly cost to you. There is no extra cost for paying monthly, as the system works out so that, during the year, there will be times when you have overpaid, and other times when you have underpaid.

The theory goes that, at the end of twelve months, everything will be straight. At that point, the gas company reassesses your likely usage over the next twelve months. They will add to this any underpayment for the year, or deduct any overpayment, and the system will then continue for another twelve months, usually based on a revised monthly payment.

The real advantage of this system is that you don't have to worry about the heavy winter months. The cost has been conveniently evened out throughout the year, and you are unlikely to be faced with any unpleasant surprises.

For council tax and water rates, the system works out slightly differently, in that your payment is normally spread over nine or ten months rather than twelve. The payments will usually start each April, which means you have a 'payment holiday' for (possibly January and) February and March – which can help to rebalance the budget after your extravagance at Christmas!

Most insurance companies will now allow you to pay premiums monthly for personal insurances such as motor and household. There will often be a small charge for this facility, but you will probably decide it is well worth paying. There is always a danger with insurance that you forget to pay the premium, and you find yourself without cover just at the point you need it most. By paying monthly, you can usually ensure that cover is maintained, without having to pay the premium in one go.

There is a disadvantage in paying monthly, as there will always be a cost. In the case of gas, electricity and telephone most of the time you are, in effect, paying in advance. You could consider working out your own monthly amounts and leaving the money in an interest-bearing, instant-access account. But the temptation would be to spend the money and then have nothing to pay the bill when it arrives. So on balance you may feel it is safer to pay as many bills as possible on a monthly basis, even though this is at some cost.

"The temptation would be to spend the money . . ."

Money within marriage

It is absolutely vital that husbands and wives develop together a proper attitude towards money. Anyone who comes to a marriage with

"What's mine is mine"

(Genesis 2:24)

(Mark 10:2–9)

(Ephesians 5:22–33)

the attitude, 'What's mine is mine,' can only expect trouble.

In Genesis we read: 'A man will leave his father and mother and be united to his wife, and they will become one flesh.' Jesus quoted these words, and added, 'So they are no longer two, but one.'

Paul, writing about the marriage relationship, again quotes these words. He spells out some of the responsibilities husbands and wives have towards each other. In addressing husbands, Paul says:

Husbands ought to love their wives as their own bodies. He who loves his wife loves himself. After all, no-one ever hated his own body, but he feeds and cares for it, just as Christ does the church.

What has this got to do with money?

Since the Bible makes it so clear that there is something very special and close about marriage, how can arguments about money come between husband and wife? The fact that money certainly does cause problems in marriages is evidence that this special relationship, instituted by God, has not been properly understood.

If there are disagreements about money within marriage, it may be because the individuals are too concerned about their own priorities, rather than being concerned with what is best for the marriage. Husband and wife, as God intended it, are one unit, and that does not leave room for selfishness.

That is not to say that marriage should stifle individual needs, or that one partner should dominate the other. But true love will always take into account the needs of the marriage as a whole.

Newlyweds will normally have developed their own attitude towards money earlier in life, and during courtship there will have been opportunity to discover the extent to which they agree on such issues. It's good to take time before marriage to explore any differences in attitude. Engaged people will be encouraged to discover that a generous spirit exists in their partner, and it is, of course, important to ensure that this spirit continues into the marriage.

". . . take into account the needs of the marriage as a whole"

*D*erek and Sheila

Derek and Sheila are aged twenty-five and twenty-three respectively. Derek has been in business for some years, and Sheila is a laboratory assistant. They have both been used to earning money and managing their own finances, including operating their own bank accounts. They have just become engaged, and plan to marry in twelve months' time.

Derek and Sheila's minister, David, arranges to counsel them on a number of occasions in preparation for their marriage, and wisely includes a session about money. Here are some of the areas David asks the couple to consider during their engagement.

Banking. Derek and Sheila each have their own accounts. Are separate accounts going to continue into marriage, or are they going to transfer to a joint account? Retaining separate accounts can encourage a possessive attitude to the money in the account, and this can cause problems particularly if there is a wide

*"Arguments
. . . concerning
who pays the
bills . . ."*

*"Some people
. . . never seem
to have any
money left"*

difference between the earnings of each partner. Furthermore, arguments can develop concerning who pays which bills. (See chapter 3 on banking.)

Giving. Derek and Sheila may not have acquired the habit of regular giving. David recognizes that if there is no discussion on this subject prior to marriage, it may be squeezed out for good. David advises them to discuss what they want to do about giving now, before they are committed to a mortgage, or have to start paying rent.

Savings. Some people always seem to manage to save money, whereas others never seem to have any money left! Again, David recognizes this basic difference and advises Derek and Sheila to investigate their respective preferences. He also warns them that, as they are about to set up home, it is possible they will be unable to save any meaningful amounts in the early years, and maybe for many years to come. But it would be useful for Derek and Sheila to discover any basic differences in attitude early on, and to talk through any such differences.

Spending. Derek has to admit that he's an impulse buyer. He will think nothing of walking into a music shop for a look around, and emerging with £50-worth of CDs. Sheila hardly ever spends money on anything other than essentials. This is the flip side to the savings coin, and again these differences need to be recognized and discussed.

David talks through this problem with Derek and Sheila, and encourages them to appreciate each other's basic differences. He advises David to develop a more measured approach to spending; he advises Sheila not to be too critical if she feels her fiancé's priorities are wrong. David stresses that the more this is discussed together before marriage, the better.

Starting a family

At one time, once married, most women would automatically cease paid employment and become housewives. This is much less likely to happen these days, and most couples wanting to rent or buy their own home will have to rely on two incomes to keep up the payments.

This trend can cause problems when the first child arrives, particularly if the couple decide that the mother (or father) is to stay at home to care for the child, at least in the early years. There is much debate concerning whether mothers should remain at home with their children, or whether they should continue to work. It is an extremely emotive issue, and a couple should pray about their plans and seek God's will.

A couple who stop to detail all the financial consequences of starting a family would probably give up the whole idea. Clearly, however, some planning is essential, and the couple will have to discuss and agree a new order of priorities.

"A couple . . . would probably give up the whole idea"

THE AGONY COLUMN

Have a go at working out your own answers before you read mine.

Q **We have a young family and my wife stays at home with the children. She now wants to start a part-time job to help us buy new furniture for the house, but I believe a mother's place is in the home. Who is right?**

A *It's not uncommon for a mother to decide to return to work after a period at home with the child or children, perhaps on a part-time basis, to help ease the strain on the domestic budget. Sometimes this is done to provide the family with some of the luxuries they have had to forgo in the early stages of having a family, or to pay for holidays or furniture.*

While this can be very useful, once the family becomes accustomed to this increase in income, it may be extremely difficult to stop. What started out as luxuries easily become life's essentials. Without straying into the sociological aspects of bringing up children, some would argue that it is just as important to have a mother at home for teenagers as it is for young children – so it would be useful to think all this through before a mother takes that initial step back to the workplace.

As to your question 'Who is right?', that is up to you as a family to work out for yourselves. Please do bear in mind that this is not a purely financial issue as far as your wife is concerned. Yes, she may be keen to help finance the furniture you need, but she may find a therapeutic value in work as well. It is just possible that your wife does not feel particularly fulfilled in her domestic role. Of course, there may be other solutions besides going back to paid work, including perhaps a greater

"What started out as luxuries easily become life's essentials"

involvement in voluntary or church-based work.

Q **My husband has a company car, and I still drive the old banger I had when we first met. Whenever he borrows my car, my husband never pays me for the petrol he uses. Isn't this a bit unreasonable?**

A *This question indicates a very 'separate' attitude towards money, and could point to some fundamental problems within the marriage – although it has to be said that there is no fixed formula to be applied, and it is up to each couple to develop their own way of organizing finances.*

Yes, it probably is unreasonable for your husband not to repay you for petrol used, if it has been discussed and agreed that that is what should happen. I suspect, however, that you have not done this, and you are expecting him to pay you when you have not actually agreed a method of dealing with these situations.

Talk the matter through. I hope you would come to the conclusion that, because all your property and money is jointly owned, it is not necessary for money to change hands. Please do not think in terms of rights for the individual, but in terms of what is right for the marriage.

CHEQUES AND BALANCES

Dealing with the bank

3

"... a bewildering choice ..."

Most people have a bank account of one kind or another. Traditionally, it has been a matter of simply choosing one of the High Street banks. More and more building societies are now offering full banking facilities, however, which presents the public with a bewildering choice.

Many bank customers are used to being able to escape the payment of bank charges as long as their account remains in credit. Banks' attitude to the making of charges changes from time to time, however, and so you may well need to obtain full details from a number of banks before making a choice.

A cheque account – otherwise known as a

current account – would seem to be a necessity for most people, although there are many different ways for these accounts to operate. You may choose to use a current account for day-to-day dealings, and a separate deposit account for any savings. Shop around the different banks and building societies in your area and see what they have to offer. You may find all you need in an interest-bearing current account, although the interest you earn on credit balances can be very low.

You will normally be given a cheque guarantee card, which will enable you to use a cheque for a purchase up to the guarantee limit. It may also function as a cash card, which will enable you to draw cash from an automated teller machine (ATM). You will be provided with a four-digit personal identification number (PIN), which you will have to memorize. You will then have to input the PIN at the ATM to withdraw the cash.

Joint accounts

If you are married there is much to be said in favour of joint current accounts, which operate on the basis that all earnings and benefits are paid into the one account, and both partners have authority to withdraw on the basis of one signature alone. This removes much of the potential possessiveness, and solves any problems over who pays the bills – they are all paid from the one, central account.

In Derek and Sheila's case, Derek earns much more than Sheila. Derek must ensure that he never uses his higher income as an excuse to have a greater say as to how the

"There has to be complete trust for a joint account to work"

". . . each partner is wanting to hold on to his or her own possessions"

(Ephesians 5:28–29)

(Ephesians 5:30)

couple's money should be spent. Similarly, there is no need for Sheila to feel somehow guilty that she is spending some of Derek's money. There is no longer any distinction of ownership – or at least there shouldn't be. Of course, as in any aspect of marriage, there has to be complete trust for a joint account to work satisfactorily.

Some couples feel that a joint account makes it difficult when buying presents for each other for birthdays, Christmas and other special occasions. This is particularly so if, for instance, a wife doesn't have any paid employment. In using the joint account to buy a gift for her husband, she feels as though she is buying him something from his own money. Many couples manage to overcome this psychological problem, but one solution is to agree that each partner will keep a small deposit account which can be topped up from time to time from the joint account, and this makes the purchase of gifts much easier.

You might have had an opportunity to look at other people's marriages. The attitudes a couple display to the ownership of money can be quite illuminating; for instance, you might notice that each partner is wanting to hold on to his or her own possessions, money or earning power. This would not seem to agree with God's way. God wants husbands and wives to work together as one body, just as the church is meant to work together as the one body of Christ: 'for we are members of his body'.

Methods of payment for goods and services

Traditionally, we have all paid for goods and services with cash – but cash is losing some of its popularity. Here is a rundown on some of the alternatives to cash.

Cheques

Most retailers will accept payment by cheque. Unless you are known personally, however, it is unlikely that your cheque will be accepted without a cheque guarantee card. This will give the retailer the security of knowing that your cheque will be honoured by your bank, up to the stated guarantee limit, even if there are insufficient funds in your account.

A cheque-book will normally be issued in conjunction with a bank 'current' account. The bank might agree to give you an overdraft facility. This simply means that the bank will allow your account balance to fall below zero, up to the amount agreed. Although overdraft facilities are quite common, did you know that it is a criminal offence to try to pay for goods or services by cheque when you know that you have insufficient funds in your account, and you have no agreed overdraft arrangement?

So how do cheques work? Let us look at an example.

Alan has a current account, and knows that his balance is only about £10. He has just banked a cheque for £100, which is a present from his grandfather. He wants to go shopping the same day, and anticipates paying £60

". . . a criminal offence . . . when you have insufficient funds in your account"

35

for a coat. Is he safe to write out a cheque for this amount on the same day he has banked the cheque for £100? Paul has no overdraft facility, and so it is important to keep his account in credit.

When you bank a cheque to your account, you do not actually have that money to spend straight away. You have to wait for the cheque to 'clear'.

Alan's grandfather banks at the Capital Bank in the High Street. Alan is with the Fortress Bank in Market Street. The Fortress returns the £100 cheque Alan has just banked back to the Capital. The Capital has to decide whether or not to honour the £100 cheque. If Alan's grandfather didn't have enough in his account to cover the cheque, the Capital may decide to 'bounce' it. This means they would send the cheque back to Alan's bank, the Fortress, saying that payment is refused.

Assuming all goes well, however, Alan's bank will know by the fourth day that the cheque has been honoured. Alan will then have 'cleared funds' in his account, which he may now spend. So it takes four 'working' days for a cheque to clear, including the day of banking. If a cheque is banked on a Monday, cleared funds should be available on the Thursday.

But what about Alan's payment of £60 for his coat? Shouldn't he wait a couple of days before spending any of the £100? Not necessarily. The £60 cheque itself will take a similar period to clear, so by the time Alan's bank has to decide whether or not to honour the cheque, it should have received the cleared funds for the £100 cheque. It would, however, be good policy to leave a gap of a day or so to be on the safe side.

Direct debits and standing orders

A direct debit is a convenient way for you to make regular payments from your account, usually for bills such as gas, electricity and telephone. Once you have signed the form to establish a direct debit, the arrangement will continue until you cancel. Sometimes the amount will need to be varied. For example, let's say you started paying the gas company £35 per month under a budget scheme, and this amount had to be increased to £45. The gas company would notify you of the increase, but there would be no need for you to sign a new form. The gas company would simply increase the amount it takes from your bank account.

Some people object to the ease at which this can be done, and feel the system is open to abuse. There are a number of safeguards, but if the operation of direct debits worries you, you could try to insist on paying by standing order. Here, the amounts payable cannot be varied without your confirming the change in writing to your bank.

Giro credits

Filling in a giro credit slip at your bank can be a convenient way of transferring money from your account to another. This may be to settle a bill, to credit money to a charity's account or for whatever purpose.

Many bills these days incorporate a giro credit slip into the tear-off portion which is used for payment. Instead of posting a cheque with the payment slip, it may be more con-

" . . . good policy to leave a gap of a day or so . . ."

venient to use the giro slip and pay over the counter at your bank.

You can settle any number of bills all at once this way. You simply total the amounts owing and write out just one cheque, payable to your own bank, for this total. You leave the rest to the bank. This can save on postage costs and bank charges, and can be safer than paying by post.

"You leave the rest to the bank"

EFTPOS

This means Electronic Funds Transfer at Point Of Sale. Common forms of EFTPOS are Delta and Switch. Some cheque guarantee cards can be used in this way – as a debit card, rather than a credit card. In other words, the amount spent is debited from your account in just the same way as a cheque.

For more information about the way debit cards work, see chapter 7 on credit and debt. Chapter 7 also takes a look at the use of credit cards.

". . . extremely useful for anyone who finds it difficult to visit a bank . . ."

Telephone banking

Many banks and building societies offer a system of telephone banking. Sometimes this involves using a tone pad with a modern telephone to send instructions to a computer. With other systems, you are able to speak to a real human being! Telephone banking can be extremely useful for anyone who finds it difficult or inconvenient to visit a bank, especially disabled people or those who work at night and sleep during the day. With some banks, you can talk to someone at 3:00am and arrange the payment of bills without even having to write out a cheque.

Accounts for children

UK bank and building-society savings accounts normally have income tax deducted from the interest paid on credit balances. Interest earned in an account in the name of a child, however, can be claimed without the tax deduction, as long as the interest earned in any one tax year does not exceed £100. (A tax year runs from 6 April one year to 5 April the next.)

To claim the interest without deduction for tax, you need to obtain a Form R85 from the bank or building society, which the parents or guardians complete on behalf of the child.

When the child reaches the age of sixteen, a new R85 has to be completed, otherwise the bank or building society will have to start deducting tax from the interest earned. Once the young person is earning sufficient to pay income tax, he or she loses the right to receive the interest without tax being deducted.

Obtaining cash abroad

Many of us are used to foreign travel, whether for business or pleasure. When is it best to use cash, travellers' cheques, or credit cards?

Let's start with cash. Without doubt, this is the most convenient; but it is not without its problems. Cash is easy to lose, and, although the instances of cash actually being stolen are few, media reports of muggings and robberies do tend to make us believe that carrying vast amounts of cash on our person is a hazardous thing to do. Even though insurance for lost cash is readily available, arranging on-the-spot replacement of stolen money is not always straightforward.

It would be easy to overlook the cost of

"Cash is easy to lose"

taking bundles of cash with you. You can probably rely on the High Street bank to provide you with a fair conversion rate, but you will still have to pay commission, usually in the region of £10 for every £1,000-worth of foreign currency. The other snag with taking cash abroad is that you have, effectively, spent the money as soon as you take delivery of the bank notes. The money has left your account, so you immediately stop earning interest on it (or start paying overdraft interest), even though the money will be used up only gradually over the period of your stay.

The problem of pre-payment also applies to travellers' cheques, although there is better protection in the event of loss. Suppliers of travellers' cheques guarantee immediate replacement, as long as you report the loss as quickly as possible. It is normal to pay a commission of 1% when purchasing the cheques (just like currency purchase), but it is also possible that a similar commission charge will be payable when you want to encash them. This problem may not arise if you can shop around. For example, if you buy American Express cheques, there will be no charge for encashment if you can find an American Express office. Experience of travelling, however, will probably tell you that you are unlikely to be passing an American Express office just when you need some cash.

Travellers' cheques are perhaps best used to pay for goods. But as the cheques are issued in precise denominations, this will mean your having to accept change in the local currency, which could cause confusion – and you will probably be in a poor position to judge if the amount given is fair. Another peculiarity

" . . . unlikely to be passing . . . just when you need some cash"

about travellers' cheques is that in some countries (for example the USA) you will find it very difficult to obtain cash; you will probably have no alternative to using the cheques in payment of goods. In Spain and Italy, if you want cash you will probably have to locate an office of the bank on which the cheques are drawn.

Particularly if you are abroad on holiday, convenience is probably more important than cost, up to a point. For this reason, travellers in Europe will probably find Eurocheques much more effective than travellers' cheques or large amounts of cash. You obtain from your bank a book of Eurocheques which are blank; you do not have to accept cheques in fixed denominations. When each cheque is used, it operates just like a UK cheque. The money does not leave your account until the cheque clears through the international banking system, because Eurocheques are not pre-purchased. Of course, you do need to make arrangements for there to be sufficient funds in your account.

Eurocheques can be used freely in Europe for the payment of goods, with each cheque being guaranteed for the local equivalent of about £100 (and you are permitted to use more than one cheque per transaction). Any bank displaying the Eurocheque symbol will encash your cheque, usually for about £100 each. The commission charge for a purchase will work out at about 1.6%, plus 45p per cheque. This is a little more expensive than the currency cost of cash or travellers' cheques, but at least you know it is the only cost of the transaction, and there are no hidden additional amounts.

"It operates just like a UK cheque"

To put the cost into perspective, if you spent £1,000 with Eurocheques, the total currency cost would be £16. In addition, though, you need to bear in mind that the rate to the pound quoted as the conversion factor will always include a 'spread' for the benefit of the Bureau de Change.

Another advantage of Eurocheques is that you can use the guarantee card with a PIN to obtain cash from certain foreign cashpoints, up to the local equivalent of £140.

One of the easiest ways of obtaining cash or paying for goods is to use a credit card. When a credit-card company receives a debit relating to an overseas transaction, they convert the currency using a mid-rate figure applying on that day, which is extremely useful, as there are no additional currency commissions. If a credit card is used to withdraw cash at home, interest is charged from the day of withdrawal; with foreign withdrawals, it is not possible for the card company to know the precise date of withdrawal, so they start the interest from the day preceding the day they receive the paperwork. Again, this is very reasonable, as it can take some days for the transaction to reach the home country.

THE AGONY COLUMN

Have a go at working out your own answers before you read mine.

 Am I not right in saying that the Bible prohibits usury, which is the same as charging interest? Banks wouldn't exist without charging interest, so why do Christians use them?

A It's true that the Bible says, 'Do not take interest of any kind . . .' (or, in the Authorized Version, 'Take thou no usury . . .'), and 'Do not charge your brother interest, whether on money or food.' But then it goes on to say, 'You may charge a foreigner interest, but not a brother Israelite.'

(Leviticus 25:36)

(Deuteronomy 23:19)

(Deuteronomy 23:20)

In the parable of the talents, the master admonishes the lazy servant by saying, 'You should have put my money on deposit with the bankers, so that when I returned I would have received it back with interest.'

(Matthew 25:27)

So back to the question. Usury does, indeed, mean the charging of interest, but this is not prohibited in all circumstances. Leviticus 25 refers to our duty towards 'a brother' who has got into difficulties. If we follow this teaching for ourselves, we would help a fellow Christian who is in need, but not charge him interest on any money we lend.

In Deuteronomy 23, again, the exhortation not to charge interest refers to 'a brother', although in this case there is no reference to the brother being in difficulties. The fact that charging interest to a foreigner was condoned would imply that charging interest as part of a business transaction is acceptable, but not if the purpose of the loan is to provide help to a friend.

So these passages would not seem to rule out a Christian's use of a bank.

" . . . we would help a fellow Christian who is in need . . ."

Q I have a small deposit in a building-society account and tax is deducted automatically from the interest earned. I recently saw an advertisement for an 'offshore' account which seemed to say that tax would not be deducted. Is there any reason why I shouldn't switch my account to save tax?

A *Yes! There are two good reasons why it would probably be unwise for you to switch. Although tax is not deducted by an offshore building society, you must still declare your interest for tax, and tax is payable by you eventually. If you do not declare the interest to the Inland Revenue, you will be committing an offence.*

You should also bear in mind that many offshore organizations are not as well regulated as UK organizations, so your money may not be as safe.

GIVING IT AWAY

| C | H | A | P | T | E | R |

Christians have a responsibility to share their income for the benefit of others and for the benefit of God's work. Giving can prove to be a sheer joy; equally, Christians can some-times develop a grudging attitude to giving, or even a guilty conscience brought about by neglecting their responsibilities.

"Giving can prove to be a sheer joy"

As with all aspects of money, we must think and pray carefully about our giving.

tithing

You may have come across the Old Testament principle of 'tithing'. A tithe is defined in the dictionary as *the tenth of the produce of land and stock* or *a levy of one-tenth*. Let's examine what the Bible says about it, so as to establish some ground rules as we think about the whole subject of giving.

Tithing was clearly intended to represent two main aspects of giving: tithing as worship, and tithing to help others. Tithing was intended to benefit the disadvantaged, and also to provide income for the religious leaders.

The following Old Testament passages help to explain these different aspects of giving.

Tithing as worship

A tithe of everything from the land, whether grain from the soil or fruit from the trees, belongs to the LORD; it is holy to the LORD . . .

(Leviticus 27:30–33)

Be sure to set aside a tenth of all that your fields produce each year . . . so that you may learn to revere the LORD your God always.

(Deuteronomy 14:22–26)

Tithing to help the poor

. . . the fatherless and the widows who live in your towns may come and eat and be satisfied . . .

(Deuteronomy 14:28–29)

Tithing for the benefit of religious leaders

And do not neglect the Levites living in your towns, for they have no allotment or inheritance of their own.

(Deuteronomy 14:27)

I give to the Levites all the tithes in Israel as their inheritance in return for the work they do while serving at the Tent of Meeting.

(Numbers 18:21)

One of the most challenging passages on the subject of giving is found in Malachi. Here, Malachi brings a rebuke from God, saying that the people were robbing God in their tithes and offerings. God had instructed them to pay a tithe to the temple, but they had been withholding these payments.

'Will a man rob God?' Yet you rob me.
But you ask, 'How do we rob you?'
'In tithes and offerings. You are under a curse —
the whole nation of you — because you are robbing
me.'

But there follows an amazing promise:

'Bring the whole tithe into the storehouse, that there may be food in my house. Test me in this,' says the LORD Almighty, 'and see if I will not throw open the floodgates of heaven and pour out so much blessing that you will not have room enough for it.'

Here is a promise we can claim for ourselves, although we should not necessarily expect the resultant blessings to come in material form. But if we are faithful to God, he will certainly bless us here on earth and in heaven.

Our response to the challenge of tithing

In contrast to the Old Testament, New Testament teaching on giving provides little indication of how much is expected of us in monetary terms. It would seem that New Testament teaching concentrates not so much on the *quantity* as on the *quality* of our giving.

We do know that Paul encouraged the early Christians to 'excel . . . in this grace of giving'. Jesus' parable of the rich fool explains about

". . . robbing God in their tithes and offerings"

(Malachi 3:8–9)

(Malachi 3:10)

"If we are faithful to God, he will certainly bless us"

(2 Corinthians 8:7)

(Luke 12:16–21) the danger of storing up wealth for the future, and his comment on the widow and her 'mite' teaches us about sacrificial giving:

As he looked up, Jesus saw the rich putting their gifts into the temple treasury. He also saw a poor widow put in two very small copper coins. 'I tell you the truth,' he said, 'this poor widow has put in more than all the others. All these people gave their gifts out of their wealth; but she out of her poverty
(Luke 21:1–4) *put in all she had to live on.'*

Jesus asks us to make our giving a private matter between ourselves and God:

... So when you give to the needy, do not announce it with trumpets, as the hypocrites do in the synagogues and on the streets, to be honoured by men. I tell you the truth, they have received
(Matthew 6:1–4) *their reward in full ...*

Perhaps there is something about living a Christian life today which has distanced us from the immediate needs around us. It may be useful to ask the same question as the lawyer in the parable of the good Samaritan:
(Luke 10:25–37) 'Who is my neighbour?'

We learn of human tragedy on the other side of the globe just as it happens. This brings the problems of thousands of people into our own homes – and usually leaves us feeling incapable of doing anything about them. In fact, we can feel so overwhelmed by the disasters of this world that not only do we make no response at all, but we also switch off from the needs of those in our immediate vicinity. We need to establish to our own satisfaction

"We can feel so overwhelmed by the disasters of this world ..."

exactly who it is we owe a duty to, and then set about putting our resolve into action.

If we mean business when it comes to organizing our giving, we could follow the principle of tithing by thinking in terms of

- giving to the church
- giving to those in need

This is a very simplistic division. It could, of course, be argued that all giving could be made through the local church, and that it should be left to the church, corporately, to decide how much to allocate to 'spiritual' and 'material' needs. Nevertheless, we shall stick with this division for now, if only to make us take account of the various aspects covered by each category.

Giving to the church
Christians will normally provide the finance to pay for church buildings, facilities and equipment, together with other costs associated with the running of a church, including those of ministers, pastors or other paid workers.

In this category we should include the financial support of other spheres of Christian work such as missionary societies and full-time workers based either at home or overseas.

Giving to those in need
It is easy to concentrate on the spiritual side of giving, and overlook our responsibilities to those in need. Even though modern society usually makes welfare provision for the less well off, there are many needy people living in our own locality. Yes, they have spiritual

"It may be that God wants to use us in the relief of their material needs . . ."

needs, but it may be that God wants to use us in the relief of their material needs as well.

*t*he mechanics of giving

Having established the biblical principle of giving, and having convinced ourselves that we need to respond, what do we do about it? Here are some options:

- To act as the Spirit leads and post off a cheque to your church, missionary society, *etc.* as you feel led.
- Collection plates.
- Bank standing orders.
- Deeds of covenant. Here, you commit yourself to providing regular support, usually over four years. The church or organization is then able to claim tax relief and enhance the value of your gifts. (See pp. 53–54.)
- Clearing-house arrangements. This is another type of covenanted giving scheme, but instead of committing yourself to the support of a particular church or organization, you covenant your giving to an independent agency. This way, you accumulate a balance in your own charitable account, and then you arrange to distribute the cash held as you wish, and when you wish. (See pp. 51–53.)

I well remember, as a young Christian, being attracted to the idea of tithing in principle. But I could never afford it. Even as a salary-earning bachelor with no commitments, there was never anything in my account at the end of the month. The result would be a somewhat half-hearted token of my love for God in the

"There was never anything in my account at the end of the month"

Sunday collection – that is, whenever I remembered to bring some cash with me.

I even had trouble during the fat months. I was full of good intentions. But one day followed another, and then another month went by, and still I had not got round to writing out that cheque and letter of encouragement I had planned.

Failure.

Then someone told me about bank standing orders, and that I could arrange for regular payments to go into a charitable clearing-house covenant scheme which would enable me to accumulate amounts in my own charit-able account, which I could then arrange to distribute in whatever direction I wanted, whenever I wanted. This was the answer to my problems.

The next step was to consider how much to give. I liked the idea of 10%, but 10% of my salary seemed just about impossible. I even-tually decided on 10% of my net salary, after all deductions – although I didn't quite manage that either. Nevertheless, I prayed about the matter and decided that I had to get the thing off the ground, and then try to increase the contributions whenever possible.

Propounders of tithing would probably have fixed views on whether we should commit 10%, and whether this should be a percentage of gross or net income. I would much rather encourage each Christian to make a concerted and prayerful effort to decide how to apply this biblical principle, rather than following a set formula. As Paul says, 'I am not commanding you, but I want to test the sincerity of your love.' Be a little wary, then, of people who want to dictate a rigid

"Still I had not got round to writing out that cheque"

(2 Corinthians 8:8)

51

system to you; the matter is between you and God.

For a young person or couple, one of life's priorities is to find somewhere to live, and that often means taking on an expensive mortgage. When deciding which house to buy, many people apply for as big a mortgage as they can afford. Or they might rent a flat or house, and make their choice on the basis of how much rent they can afford. This strategy can make it extremely difficult to find room in the domestic budget for any giving.

Although you've got to house yourself and perhaps a family too, once you relegate your giving to the leftovers, it is difficult to rectify the situation later on. It can take many years for your budget to regain any hint of a surplus, during which time you may have started a family. You may have been used to two salaries, and so when you are down to just one salary, even temporarily, the pressure is back once more.

Once you've been operating a clearing-house system for a few months, you become accustomed to the regular amount leaving your bank account. Perhaps it would be an exaggeration to say you hardly miss it, but it is certainly true that it turns out to be easier than you had imagined.

Then you decide to make a gift. What a joy it is to be able to request a cheque, drawn on your trust account, and made payable to your church, an evangelist, a missionary society – or whatever you choose. The money is there. You have already committed it. You don't have to re-budget the domestic finances. Even if you are feeling particularly poor at the end of the month, you can still make the gifts.

" . . . once you relegate your giving to the leftovers . . ."

"Even if you are feeling particularly poor at the end of the month . . ."

It is difficult to describe the joy of being able to send off a gift, even when you are feeling the pressure of coping with the economic realities of everyday living. Once you have made the decision to set a percentage of your income to one side, it is great to know that it is there for you to distribute whenever you feel the time is right, rather than being dictated by circumstances.

You may also like to think about making regular monthly gifts by standing order out of your clearing-house account to your church, missionary society or full-time worker. This would be especially useful if you develop an interest in supporting an individual. He or she will certainly appreciate receiving your support on a reliable, monthly basis.

*h*ow a deed of covenant works

You complete a deed, which is a legal agreement to make a series of payments out of taxed income (usually monthly or annually) for a period of more than three years (usually four). The contributions can be for the 'advancement of religion' and for the benefit of registered charities, recognized places of worship, Christian workers or evangelists.

The charity (or clearing house) will be able to reclaim from the Inland Revenue tax at the basic rate, currently 25%.

For a basic-rate taxpayer, and assuming a tax rate of 25%, this means that every £75 given by covenant is worth £100 to the charity. (The amount the charity receives is £100, but this costs you only £75, which is £100 less

25%.) If you pay tax at 40% the same applies, but your total tax bill is reduced by a further £15.

Gift-Aid Scheme. This allows a charity to reclaim tax on a single gift of £250 net with the minimum of formality, and with no obligation to make regular contributions.

*h*ow to use a clearing-house covenant scheme

Obtain information on facilities available (see 'Where to get help' at the end of the book). Write to the agency of your choice and request details on how to open an account.

"Decide how much you can sensibly commit . . ."

Decide how much you can sensibly commit to a regular arrangement, then complete the standing order and deed of covenant. This will normally be a commitment over four years.

When you want to make a gift, simply write to the agency requesting a cheque made out to the church, society or other beneficiary. This will normally be posted to you, so that you can send it off with your own covering letter. Some agencies will arrange direct payments for you if you so wish; others operate a voucher system so that you send the charity a voucher which the charity returns to the agency for payment.

". . . regular automatic payments by standing order on your behalf"

You can arrange for the agency to make regular automatic payments by standing order on your behalf.

The agency will see to the tax reclaim for you. Once this is received, it will be credited to your clearing-house account, and will be available for you to distribute as you wish.

What if you enter into a deed of covenant, but your financial circumstances change, and you cannot afford to make the agreed payments? Although, when you sign a deed of covenant, you are entering into a legal agreement, in practice it is not difficult to gain release from the arrangement if you cannot afford to keep the arrangement going. The agreement made is between you and the church, charity or clearing house, and so you would have to write, stating the reason you wish to discontinue. The organization would have no reason to force you to continue, and so you would find it fairly easy to stop the payments. In practice, you are not likely to be faced with any tax reclaim.

fund-raising

The availability of covenanting raises some questions about the methods churches use to raise funds. Perhaps if all Christians accepted the principle of tithing, the churches would have no need to resort to money-raising activities of any sort. Many people feel that some of these activities are worthwhile in themselves, but I would suggest that a prayerful approach to the challenge to all Christians to give would see a transformation in churches and missionary organizations.

In fact, I have always felt a little uneasy about collection plates being circulated in open meetings, as if we were expecting guests from outside the fellowship to contribute to the Lord's work. Surely that is our responsibility. Let outsiders know that we are interested in them, not their money.

" . . . a little uneasy about collection plates . . ."

Having said that, even though I have a personal preference for regular giving by 'mechanical' means, such as a bank standing order linked to a deed of covenant, that is not to say that there is no place at all for the collection plate. I know that many Christians look forward to that part of the church service when they can prayerfully commit their giving to God via the collection. It is a part of their worship.

Most churches operate an 'envelope' scheme. This is another way of committing yourself to a regular level of contribution, but in this case the amount you are giving is placed in an envelope which you put into the collection plate on Sunday. This is another form of covenanted giving, but is less mechanical for those who prefer the more traditional collection.

One final comment about deeds of covenant. Think of a small to medium-sized missionary society, whose annual income from its supporters comes to £200,000. Almost all the gifts received come as cheques in the post. If, instead, just 50% of the donated income came via deeds of covenant, this would release over £30,000 of reclaimed tax to be used for the Lord's work.

*M*issionary societies

Most missionary societies rely on the gifts they receive from the Christian community to survive. Very few societies have sufficient funds to enable them to operate for more than a short period using just their own resources. You may well feel, as many Christians do, that there should be no need for missionary societies at all; shouldn't all Christian workers simply rely on God to meet all their needs?

Perhaps there is something to be said for the Christian church reverting to such a system. There are, however, considerable advantages for many full-time workers who have the opportunity to work under the umbrella of a society. Not only does the society handle their support, but it can be an enormous help in many other practical ways. And, like it or not, there can be no doubt about the dramatic impact which many societies make in the worldwide work of God.

Therefore, although we have to think through what financial support we should be providing for Christian work carried out locally, and through our own church, you may feel that it would be appropriate for you to support one or more missionary societies, either as a private individual, or through your church. Workers in the mission field need support from those of us with income from secular jobs.

So plan your giving. See what the Bible has to say on the subject, and pray about your own response. Try to incorporate your giving into your domestic budget (see chapter 2).

"Shouldn't all Christian workers simply rely on God to meet all their needs?"

THE AGONY COLUMN

Have a go at working out your own answers before you read mine.

". . . just another form of gambling . . ."

Q **What about raffles? I think they are an interesting and effective way of raising money, but other Christians I know object, saying it is just another form of gambling.**

A *Looking first at the legal angle, raffles are subject to strict control under the Betting, Gaming and Lotteries Act 1963. So it would be difficult to argue that a raffle is not a form of gambling, because the law quite clearly states that it is.*

You will have to consider for yourself the wisdom of the 'occasional flutter'. Most Christians, if asked, would probably say they do not approve of gambling, and yet a fairly high percentage of those asked would, I imagine, have no objection to purchasing a raffle ticket now and then. This is not too surprising; after all, life is full of contradictions.

What complicates this issue is the fact that, invariably, the raffle is for a good cause and one which we want to support. For anyone who is unhappy about raffles, this presents a conflict: do we stick to our guns and refuse to buy a ticket, or do we put our reservations to one side in the knowledge that we are assisting a worthwhile charitable objective?

My own experience of raffles has always been outside the church context. For example, if I am attending a school fair, it is not unusual to be met at the entrance with a request to buy a raffle ticket in aid of the school fund. A refusal to buy a ticket can make me feel most unreasonable, particularly if the seller points out that the school fund is for the benefit of the whole school, my own children included.

There have been times when I have given in

and purchased a ticket but, to be honest, I have never been happy doing this. Recently, I have started refusing a ticket, but offering a small donation to the cause. This produces an interesting variety of blank looks and incredulity, but can also provide a useful opportunity for me to explain my position.

In the church context, I would find it difficult to justify the use of a raffle under any circumstances. It is up to the church members to support the work of the church, and to do it happily and willingly. If it is necessary to generate support by appealing to the motive of personal gain, then the church leaders have some serious thinking to do.

" . . . an interesting variety of blank looks . . ."

Q **I would like to support an evangelist. I would like to do this under a deed of covenant, but he does not work for an organization. What is the best way to arrange this?**

A *You should approach one of the clearing houses listed in 'Where to get help' at the end of this book. Explain to them what you want to achieve. They will ask you a few questions about the individual you want to support, and they may be able to arrange a deed of covenant with you. This covenant will be an agreement between you and the clearing house; in turn, they will pass your gifts on to the evangelist.*

SAVINGS, INVESTMENTS AND MORTGAGES

5

You might think this chapter is all a bit hypothetical for you; you have no money to invest, so what's the point of reading about investments?

From a purely secular point of view, you could say that it is the investing of money which keeps our society going. Large public companies which are quoted on the Stock Exchange rely on investment for their very existence through their share capital.

It is not unusual for governments to borrow money so that they can carry out all the public expenditure they have promised to undertake.

Pension funds invest in a wide variety of investments so that the money in the fund may grow, which enables the fund to pay the income to the pensioners.

Insurance companies have to keep vast reserves so that they can pay claims when disaster strikes, and these reserves are normally invested in some way.

So you can hardly avoid having something to do with investments at some stage of your life, even if only indirectly.

Margaret is twenty-eight and single. She works as a legal secretary and receives a good salary. In fact, she receives much more in salary than she needs for her usual living expenses, and she has arranged regular giving to her church fellowship and some other Christian organizations.

So what financial plans should Margaret make for the future?

Where is Margaret going to live? She has no plans to marry at present, but feels it is about time she left her parents and established her own home. Should she rent or buy? If she is going to buy, how should she go about getting a mortgage, and what sort of mortgage would be suitable?

What should Margaret do about any surplus income? Should she be persuaded to start a life assurance scheme? Should she be investing for her pension?

Margaret decides to buy a small house as she feels this would be a wise investment for the future, and she does not like the idea of paying rent. That to her would be 'dead money'.

So Margaret goes off to the building society. She decides to ask for some general advice about mortgages before looking for a suitable purchase.

"You can hardly avoid having something to do with investments"

The building-society manager is very helpful, and starts by making sure that Margaret is contemplating buying property for the right reasons. 'If you are buying only because you think it is a good investment, think again,' he warns. 'These days, house prices do not necessarily increase. Go ahead if what you really want is somewhere to live. That way, if the value of your home increases over the years, you can count that as a bonus.'

The manager then goes on to explain the different mortgages available.

Normal repayment mortgage. This is sometimes called an 'annuity' mortgage. The manager explains to Margaret that she would borrow a capital sum over a fixed period, usually twenty-five years. The building society would work out what the monthly cost would be, but this cost would change whenever interest rates changed. Part of what is paid each month is the interest due to the building society; the other part repays a small amount of the sum borrowed. In this way, everything will be paid off by the end of twenty-five years. No ifs or buts. At the end of twenty-five years, Margaret would, at last, own the house outright.

Endowment mortgage. This is a little more complicated. Again, the monthly cost is split in two ways. The amount paid to the building society this time consists of interest only. There is no payment to reduce the amount of capital outstanding, which means the monthly payments to the building society are much lower than with a normal repayment mortgage.

Margaret would, however, have to take out an *endowment policy* with an insurance com-

" . . . you can count that as a bonus"

"Margaret would, at last, own the house outright"

pany. The intention would be that, over the twenty-five years, the policy would grow so that it would pay off the amount originally borrowed from the building society. In the meantime, the endowment policy would contain life insurance which would pay the mortgage off if Margaret died before the end of the twenty-five-year term. Margaret would find that this arrangement would cost more each month than a repayment mortgage.

So why do an endowment mortgage, if it costs more? Well, the idea is that the endowment should actually pay out more than the amount originally borrowed, providing Margaret with some extra cash for herself. It would, however, be difficult to predict exactly how much extra the policy would provide, as who knows how well the insurance company is going to do with its investments over such a long period? Also, there is a bewildering variety of endowments available, and the success of an endowment mortgage will very much depend on the quality of the insurance company and the type of endowment purchased.

Margaret eventually decides to go for the more traditional repayment mortgage. She is not all that interested in paying a higher monthly amount in exchange for the hope of an unspecified payout in twenty-five years' time. Furthermore, Margaret is not interested in life insurance, as she has no dependants.

Before starting the house-hunting, Margaret has to know what her price range is going to be. She has managed to save £5,000, and wants to know how much she will be allowed to borrow.

The building-society manager explains that

"Who knows how well the insurance company is going to do?"

he would be prepared to lend up to $2^1/_2$ times Margaret's annual gross income (before deduction for tax, national insurance, *etc.*), but subject to a maximum of 90% of the house valuation. (Some building societies will agree to granting a higher mortgage based on a higher multiplier, perhaps as high as $3^1/_2$ times salary.)

Margaret's salary is £15,000 *p.a.*, so she can borrow up to £37,500. She sees a property advertised for £38,000. She qualifies for a £34,200 mortgage on it, *i.e.* 90% of the value. This means she has to use up £3,800 of her savings, though another £300-£400 will be needed for legal and valuation fees. (These amounts vary with the purchase price of the house.) She also has to pay a 'mortgage indemnity' premium (in her case £400) to the building society. Such a premium is normally payable for loans which exceed 75% of the valuation, and the insurance provides some protection for the building society in the event that the customer is unable to keep up the repayments.

Margaret now works out a new budget of her income and expenditure and concludes that she can just about afford the repayments. But she also realizes that she would be in great difficulty if she were to lose her job or become ill. So the building-society manager arranges a redundancy and sickness insurance which Margaret will be able to pay monthly.

Where does the building society obtain the money to lend to Margaret?

The answer, of course, is savings. If it wasn't for the fact that other people put their savings into building-society accounts, there would be no money to lend. Here, then, is another example of investments helping to make the economy of the country, as well as of the individual, work.

Some years pass. Margaret, who is still single, finds that she is managing to keep up her payments to the building society more comfortably than previously, and she decides she should invest part of her surplus income each month. Here are details of the investments Margaret considers.

Pension

Margaret's employer operates a pension scheme, and Margaret has been a member of the scheme for six years. She has never understood much about this arrangement, so she makes it her business to find out some facts.

It comes as a surprise to Margaret that her employer pays a sum equal to 4% of her salary into the scheme each month. On top of this, Margaret herself pays 3%, and this part is deducted from her pay. This means that 7% of her salary is being put to one side each month to provide a pension on retirement. This pension will be in addition to the State pension.

Margaret learns that there is a facility for making extra payments to boost her pension. These are known as Additional Voluntary Contributions (AVCs). This would be extremely useful for Margaret, especially as AVCs attract tax relief – in other words, the Government will refund the tax paid on any income which is invested in an AVC, up to certain limits. Margaret has to bear in mind, however, that money invested in this way becomes inaccessible, as it has to remain

"... AVCs attract tax relief ..."

within the pension scheme until retirement age.

Putting surplus income into a pension arrangement is always going to be a good investment, for two reasons. First, there is the tax relief on the contributions; secondly, the insurance company which runs the scheme does not have to pay tax on the pension fund. These tax advantages provide a considerable help in making sure the fund performs well over the years.

Had Margaret not been a member of her employer's pension scheme, she could have started her own personal pension plan, which would benefit from the same tax concessions.

Insurance-company savings schemes

Margaret notices how many insurance-company advertisements there are in the paper. But how can she find out which savings schemes are suitable for her?

Margaret is recommended to consult an insurance broker, one who specializes in life insurance and savings. This way, she can know she is dealing with someone who will provide an impartial service. When discussing savings schemes and investments, it is always important to establish at the outset whether or not the advisor is independent. If the person is a 'tied agent', he or she represents one insurance company only, and so can recommend only the products of that one company. Someone who calls himself or herself an insurance broker *has* to be independent, however, and can survey the whole insurance and investment market, and then recommend the insurance company and product best suited to your individual needs.

"How can she find out which savings schemes are suitable for her?"

Anyone who is being guided on investment matters should, however, remember that it is usually only by the payment of commission that the broker or adviser makes a living. No sale, no income. All advisers are required by law to put your interests before their own, but it pays to be cautious, and there is no harm in seeking advice from more than one source. For example, you could listen to the advice available from your bank or building society, and then compare this with what an insurance broker has to say.

As a general rule, it is best not to make a decision on the spot. Leave the decision for a few days, and then go back with a list of any questions you may have thought of in the meantime.

How do you go about finding a good adviser? Look under 'Insurance brokers' in the *Yellow Pages*. Brokers are particularly well regulated and can generally be relied upon to put your interests first. You will be able to tell from the advertisements whether individual firms specialize in general insurance, or life and pensions. There is no point asking a specialist motor insurance broker about investments, so, if in doubt, ask.

Many independent advisers are not insurance brokers, but are regulated by the Personal Investment Authority (PIA). The PIA's address and telephone number are under 'Where to get help' at the end of this book. They will provide names and addresses of firms local to you.

Another organization, IFA Promotions, will also provide you with information on suitably qualified advisers. Again, their details are at the end of this book.

"How do you go about finding a good advisor?"

67

Insurance-company products come in all shapes and sizes, with a confusing array of names and descriptions. There is no particular need to be aware of all these products in order to make a sensible choice, as it is much more important to make sure you are going to the right person for advice. Nevertheless, it may be useful to know some basic details of the savings schemes which crop up most frequently.

Endowments

A regular premium, usually monthly, is paid for a period agreed at the outset, for example twenty years. Your life is insured for a set sum during the period, at the end of which you expect to receive the 'sum assured', which is paid to you tax free.

There are three main types of endowment: non-profit, with-profit and unit-linked. There are very few occasions when a *non-profit endowment* should be considered, as all you receive is the guaranteed sum assured on maturity, which does nothing to offset the effects of inflation.

"There are three main types of endowment"

A *with-profit endowment* is invested in various ways, mainly stocks and shares. One attractive feature of these policies is that, once your policy has acquired a 'bonus' (which represents the profit), it cannot be taken away from you, even if future investment performance is poor. This helps to make the investment fairly safe and secure.

A *unit-linked endowment* is also an investment into stocks and shares, although there is no safety net as there is with the with-profit endowment bonus system. After your policy has been growing well over the years, there may be a collapse in the stock market just before the policy matures. Unit-linked policies often out-perform the safer with-profit policies, but there is more risk attached to this approach.

Whole life policies
These are similar to endowments, except that they pay out on death only. This is an open-ended arrangement under which the policy will simply continue until you die, whenever that may happen to be. If you want a policy which will produce a lump sum in your lifetime, rather than just on your death, choose an endowment rather than a whole life policy.

If you want to insure your life for a specific purpose, such as to provide financial protection for a family, or to cover a mortgage, ask your insurance broker about term insurance or family income benefit cover. These policies pay out nothing at all if you survive the period of the policy, but provide remarkably inexpensive cover in the meantime. This sort of policy is of no interest at all to Margaret, as she is not married and has no dependants.

"remarkably inexpensive cover . . ."

Unit trusts
Here is another example of an investment into a range of stocks and shares. Some, but not all, unit trusts will accept monthly contributions. Again, this can be a somewhat volatile investment, and should be viewed as a long-term commitment – over a number of years rather than months. Having said that, with a unit-trust investment you do not have to sign up over a specified term, so you have more flexibility and more access to your money than you do with a life assurance policy.

Personal Equity Plans (PEPs)

These, too, are somewhat speculative, although the investments grow in a tax-free fund, rather like a pension fund.

The performance of PEPs and unit trusts has been mixed in recent years and should, therefore, be considered only by people who are willing to take the risk.

Tax Exempt Special Savings Accounts (TESSAs)

These accounts are available at most High Street banks and building societies. There are limits on how much you can invest, and, to obtain the benefit of the tax exemption, you have to leave the money in the account for five years. TESSAs can be very useful for people who know they are unlikely to require access to their money for some time. There is no speculative element to TESSAs, as they are simply savings accounts with no tax to pay on the interest.

They are not, however, suitable for people who do not pay income tax. Non-taxpayers can apply for interest earned in *any* bank and building-society account to be paid gross, without deduction for income tax. To apply, complete Form R85, available from the bank or building society. Non-taxpayers should also obtain details of the accounts available from National Savings; leaflets are available at Post Offices.

Margaret is now in her fifties, and learns that an aunt has died and left her £10,000 in her will. Margaret decides to treat this as if it were part of her ordinary income, and therefore allocates a percentage towards her Chris-

". . . savings accounts with no tax to pay on the interest . . ."

tian giving. She then decides to invest the balance and, once again, turns to her insurance broker for advice.

Again, the quality of advice is all-important. Risk is the important issue here. It's all very well getting carried away with the idea of making money grow by investing in stocks and shares, but there is always the risk that the amount invested could reduce in value rather than increase.

The following table shows the risk attaching to most of the popular investments which investment advisers will recommend, with risk valued on a scale of 1 to 10, with 1 being non-speculative, and 10 being extremely speculative.

This should be used as a checklist for any recommendations you receive. Even though you will not understand what some of the investments are, the table will act as a useful warning against some of the more risky investments.

"There is always the risk that the amount invested could reduce in value"

Type of investment	Risk
Bank deposit account	1
Building-society account	1
National Savings account (Post Office)	1
Insurance-company investment bond	8
Insurance bond with guaranteed preservation of capital	4
Insurance guaranteed income bond	2
Unit trust	9
Investment trust	10
Broker bond	10
Stocks and shares	10
Tax Exempt Special Savings Account (TESSA)	1
Personal Equity Plan (PEP)	8

(A broker bond is an insurance-company investment bond, but you provide your broker with an authority to switch from one fund to another. This can produce an enhanced investment return, but the risks are fairly high.)

The golden rule is to make sure you are receiving good advice; if necessary, consult more than one adviser. You must ask the adviser to spell out just how much risk is being taken with your money. You must also make sure you understand everything before you commit yourself.

In 1986, the world's stock markets had never looked so strong. People were beginning to believe that an investment into stocks and shares was a recipe for quick and easy profits. Then came the worldwide collapse of equity markets, and millions of pounds were wiped off the value of people's investments.

" . . . a recipe for quick and easy profits . . ."

This was not so bad for those who had been investing for some time, because all they lost was some of the profit they had been building up. But it was a disaster for those investors who had only recently gone into stocks and shares, perhaps for the first time in their lives. Such people had expected their capital to appreciate, and yet the value may have fallen by 50% or more overnight. Expectations were so high that the risk factor had been ignored.

Margaret decides to make an investment in stocks and shares, but she does this through a unit trust, and invests only £2,500. She leaves the rest in her building-society account for maximum peace of mind.

Each investor will have his or her own attitude to risk. In Margaret's case, she did not get so carried away that she risked the security of her whole investment, keeping the bulk in the safe haven of the building society.

Ethical investments
Some investors are attracted to the concept of investing in the stock market through an insurance-company fund or unit trust, but wish to ensure that the fund managers will not invest their money in industries they would rather avoid, such as the arms trade. It is for this reason that the 'ethical' funds have been started, and your broker should be able to provide details on request. Despite the investment restrictions placed on such funds, there is no evidence that the investment performance is impaired.

THE AGONY COLUMN

Have a go at working out your own answers before you read mine.

Q **If people buy shares in the hope that they will increase in value, so that they can then sell at a higher price, isn't this just an up-market way of gambling? Is it any better than putting money on the horses?**

A *This can be a difficult ethical question for Christians. The answer is to be found in examining the motive for investing in stocks and shares.*

It is the shareholders who keep the companies in existence. Their investment carries out a most useful role, and in return they receive a dividend. On top of this, if the company is going well, the value of the shareholding will increase (and if the company falls on hard times, the value will decrease). This is only fair, as the shareholders are in fact the owners of the company.

If the investor's motives for buying the shares are to provide capital for industry, and to obtain a reasonable return on his or her money in exchange, knowing that the value of the shares will fluctuate in line with the fortunes of the company, then that would seem to be perfectly acceptable. In reality, few people will buy shares just to help the company, but there is nothing inherently wrong in buying shares.

Some investors will buy shares not so much to obtain a dividend as to speculate that the share price will rise rather than fall. If that is the only motive, then I would have to accept that this is more akin to gambling, and should raise questions in the mind of the Christian investor.

But I should add that this is a matter for the individual investor to settle to his or her own satisfaction, rather than for green-eyed onlookers, who wish they had the money to invest, and end up criticizing those who do.

"Shouldn't we all be selling what we have?"

Q **Why do Christians save, when it is quite clear from the Bible that we are not to store up wealth? In fact, shouldn't we all be selling what we have and following Jesus?**

A *Yes, I do think we should all be ready to sell everything we have, if we are called to do so. It can be possible for us to respond in* this way, as long as we have not put too heavy a reliance on our worldly wealth.

But God treats us all as individuals, and it is up to each of us to settle such matters before him. It seems clear that some Christians are indeed called to live without many of the worldly comforts most of us are used to; many of us are not so called. The question we must ask ourselves is whether we would be prepared to give up everything if we felt that was what God wanted us to do.

The challenge of Jesus' illustration about the rich man who stored up his wealth in barns lies in our reason for saving. If we save a little for our old age, so that we don't become a liability to others, that is one thing; if we are greedily amassing as much wealth as possible, with little regard to the needs of others, then that is something else. While we should make sensible provision for the future, and for others who may be dependent on us, we must always remember that what God has given us is not to be used just to make life more comfortable for ourselves.

" . . . prepared to give up everything if we felt that was what God wanted . . ."

(Luke 12:16–21)

ALL ABOUT INSURANCE

No one person understands everything there is to know about insurance, and a little knowledge is a dangerous thing. The general rule about insurance is to assume nothing and always seek advice.

The purpose of this chapter is to provide a few pointers to prevent your falling into one or more of the many traps.

Life insurance

It is a fact that most life cover is taken out only because of a salesperson's powers of persuasion, or because a lender, such as a building society, has insisted that some cover should exist.

The trouble with responding to an approach from a salesperson is that you can often end up buying cover which is either too expensive or inappropriate.

First, consider whether you need life insurance at all. Are you married or single? If you are single, is there anyone who relies on you financially? If not, there is little point in arranging life cover. Some sales-people are quite prepared to sell costly life assurance schemes to young, single people on the basis that the cover should be bought now while premiums are cheap, and that the cover gets more expensive with the passing of each birthday. But most people who buy as a result of such arguments end up wasting money, and it is usually better to forget about life cover until it is actually needed.

Most people would regard it as useful to have some life insurance as soon as they marry – although, again, cover may be unnecessary until children come along. If cover is required, it is important to consider very carefully just how much is needed. For instance, a husband may think that £100,000 is a lot of life cover. But if he were to die, leaving his wife to bring up a young family on her own, £100,000 wouldn't go as far as you would think. In such circumstances, a young widow would want to retain the value of the capital and live off the interest. At, say, 5% interest, this sum would produce an annual income of only £5,000.

Many young couples have little need of elaborate savings schemes, because they should always ensure that any savings remain

"£100,000 wouldn't go as far as you would think"

accessible. In other words, there is little point tying up money in, say, a twenty-five-year life policy, when the priority may be to save up for a deposit to put on a house. If the savings are locked in, they will be of little practical use. So a young couple should try to arrange whatever life cover is needed on a 'term' basis. This means that the amount of cover is payable only in the event of death within the term selected; if death does not occur, the policy pays nothing. More complicated savings schemes, which usually combine life cover with a savings arrangement (such as an endowment), can usually be left until later in life.

People are usually surprised to learn just how inexpensive straightforward life insurance is. Andrew (aged twenty-four) and Sarah (twenty-two) are expecting their first child, and Sarah plans to give up work. They can buy a term policy which will pay out £100,000 in the event that either of them dies within twenty-five years. This level of cover can be obtained for under £25 per month. As circumstances change, the policy can simply be cancelled or updated.

*M*otor insurance

The basic choice is whether to insure for comprehensive or third party, fire and theft. The main difference between the two covers is that whereas you can claim for damage done to your own car under a comprehensive policy, you can't if the cover has been restricted to third party, fire and theft.

Motor insurance probably produces the

highest number of problems and misunderstandings. These usually arise because the policy-holder has not understood the nature of the cover in the first place.

It is most important to fill in the proposal form very carefully. It is your responsibility to tell the insurance company about anything which is 'material' (anything the insurance company should know about so that it can decide whether to grant insurance, and at what premium).

For instance, the proposal form will ask if you have received any motoring convictions. You may have forgotten all about the fine for speeding three years ago, but if you don't declare this on the proposal form, this could cause problems when you come to make a claim. Failing to declare a 'material' fact can entitle the insurance company to refuse the claim.

" . . . the fine for speeding three years ago . . ."

Another question will ask about previous accidents. You must insert details of all previous accidents, even those which were not your fault.

Be careful to apply for the 'class of use' which is needed in your case. For instance, if you apply for social and domestic use only, but have an accident while you are running an errand for your employer, cover will not apply.

Do not rely on your motor policy to cover items in the car, such as coats, cameras or Christmas shopping. Even if the policy does provide a measure of cover for these things, a claim will mean that you lose your no-claims bonus, so it is hardly worth claiming. Personal items should be insured separately. (See below.)

" . . . take adequate precautions to prevent a loss"

One final warning about motor insurance. There is a clause in any insurance contract which states that it is your responsibility to take adequate precautions to prevent a loss. If you leave your car unattended with the keys in the ignition, for instance, don't be surprised if your insurer refuses to pay when the car is stolen. Before you say that you would never leave the keys in, what about when you are at the petrol station? Many people leave the keys in place when they go to pay for the petrol, and insurance companies have been known to refuse to pay out for cars stolen on such occasions.

*h*ome insurance

There are two types of home policy: one to cover the buildings, and the other for the contents and personal belongings. The most important aspect to watch is that you have covered yourself for the full amount.

Buildings
The amount of insurance you need is dictated by the cost to rebuild. For example, think of a house which has suffered from an extensive fire and is not capable of being repaired. The homeowner would expect his insurance company to pay not only the cost of building a new home, but also any additional costs such as demolishing the remains of the house and clearing the site. It would also be necessary to employ an architect to draw up new plans. So it is useful to obtain some advice about rebuilding costs, as the amount of insurance

you need is not necessarily in line with the market value of the property.

Ask your insurance broker to obtain a copy of the free leaflet issued by the Association of British Insurers called *Buildings Insurance for Home Owners*. This will explain how to go about calculating the 'sum insured' properly.

If you fit bedroom furniture, or a new kitchen, you will need to add the replacement value of this to the buildings policy (not the contents policy). Similarly, you will have to allow for any extensions or the addition of a conservatory.

" . . . how to go about calculating the 'sum insured' . . ."

Contents

Most contents policies now provide 'new for old' cover. The older type of cover, known as 'indemnity', used to mean that on any claims settlement the insurer would deduct an amount for wear and tear. Under a 'new for old' policy, this deduction is not made, except for items of clothing and linen and sometimes bicycles and sports items. This means that you have to cover your contents for the full cost of replacing everything at today's prices, no matter how old things are.

If you under-insure either the buildings or the contents, you will not receive the full amount you expect under any claims payment. So it pays to give the matter serious thought and take expert advice.

Sometimes it can be difficult to know which items to insure under the buildings policy, and which under contents. As a general rule, anything you would leave behind, were you to move, should be considered as part of the building; anything else can be treated as contents.

There are many ways of obtaining insurance, but it usually pays to consult an insurance broker. An intermediary can call himself an insurance broker only if he is properly qualified and registered. See 'Where to get help' at the end of this book for the address and telephone number of the British Insurance and Investment Brokers Association, who will be able to let you have the names and addresses of local insurance brokers.

THE AGONY COLUMN

Have a go at working out your own answers before you read mine.

"Isn't this evidence of lack of faith in God's provision?"

Q If a Christian decides to take out insurance, isn't this evidence of lack of faith in God's provision?

A Strictly speaking, I suppose I have to agree with you. In the ideal Christian community, the strong would help the weak, and those who suffered loss would be helped by the rest of the group. But Christians usually have no choice but to live in the world as it is, and modern society prefers to cater for the unexpected by purchasing insurance. As Christians are part of this same world, it would be difficult to adopt a different approach.

Of course, there are occasions when you have no choice. The law requires you to insure against any damage or injury you may cause while driving a vehicle, and to take out liability insurance if you employ anyone. And banks and building societies will normally insist that you insure a property on which you arrange a mortgage, and may also insist that your life is insured.

The principle of insurance is not much different from living within a commune; the misfortunes of the few are shared by the majority. Christians, by their payment of premiums, are simply joining in with the rest of society and sharing in the same pool of risk.

". . . sharing in the same pool of risk . . ."

It would be good to think, however, that Christians demonstrated a desire to go one step further. I know of a case where a man in his fifties died unexpectedly, and left very little life cover for his wife and young family. Sadly, there was little practical help from the church, and this resulted in the family having to accept a dramatic fall in their living conditions.

This demonstrates the current difficulty, in that the church doesn't seem to know where its duty lies in such circumstances. In the light of this uncertainty, it is only sensible to avail oneself of whatever insurance is available.

But we can't leave the matter there, because the questioner was talking about relying on God, not an imperfect Christian community. We know that God wants us to rely on him, but to what extent should we make use of modern methods to protect us against the unforeseen events of life? If God uses his people in the provision of others' needs, what should Christians do when the church seems to make an inadequate response? Over to you!

"We know that God wants us to rely on him, but . . ."

Q It says in the Bible that Christians are not to sue each other. What happens if I am driving my car, and am hit by a car

being driven by another Christian. Is it right for me to claim against the Christian for the damage caused to my car?

A The easy way out, if you have a comprehensive policy, is to claim for your damage under your own policy, and leave the respective insurance companies to make their own arrangements concerning responsibility. If it is shown that the other driver was at fault, and was properly insured, you should not have to suffer a reduction in your no-claims bonus.

But does this constitute suing a brother or sister in Christ? I suppose you could argue that it does, since a claim cannot be established against another motorist without there being proof of legal responsibility. But the whole process is reasonably clinical, and it is highly unlikely that the other motorist would be in any way offended by the fact that you have asked your insurance company to represent your interests.

These things do not, however, always work out so easily. As anyone who has had a motoring accident will know, it is not always agreed who is actually responsible for the accident. Christians should do their best to make an honest assessment regarding their own responsibility, and try not to assert their rights to the extent that two Christians get involved in an unseemly dispute.

Think about this: what would you do if a Christian motorist damaged your car, had no insurance, and was in no position to pay you for the damage caused?

CREDIT AND DEBT

How it all begins

7

| C | H | A | P | T | E | R |

My wife and I were doing our weekly shop one Friday night, accompanied by our two children. My young son, James, was watching with great interest as a woman routed through the frozen-food cabinet. She lifted a packet out of the freezer, and said aloud to herself, 'Oh, diced rabbit,' clearly thinking this would represent a welcome treat for her family.

James wasn't impressed with this, as he contemplated the feelings of his own pet rabbit back home.

He could contain himself no longer. 'Diced rabbit? You might just as well call it chopped bunny!'

". . . the feelings of his own pet rabbit back home . . ."

85

This had a profound effect on the woman, who solemnly placed the packet back in the freezer cabinet, saying, 'I couldn't possibly buy this now!'

So what's the difference between diced rabbit and chopped bunny? Nothing at all, of course, except that one phrase has a more emotional connotation than the other. Diced rabbit is the sanitized term preferred by civilized society, because it succeeds in removing the reality from our minds. Unless we are vegetarians, we enjoy our meat even though we are fully aware of its origins – but we prefer not to be reminded of those too often.

And that is why we use the term 'credit' instead of the true term 'debt'.

There is something very alluring about credit. If I successfully apply for a credit card, this makes me feel I have achieved something. Someone somewhere has decided that I am worthy to have this credit facility. Paying cash is only for those who cannot be trusted. But I have achieved the ability to have credit, which places me in a class above the rest.

Now I can visit shops and pay for goods on credit, in the knowledge that presenting my credit card is evidence of the fact that I have status, and people will look up to me, knowing that I have proved my worth. And when I earn enough, I can apply for a gold card, which is even further evidence that I am a cut above the rest of the bunch. Then, I will have truly arrived.

"Then, I will have truly arrived"

This is, of course, total nonsense. But it does illustrate the pulling power of credit. Some booklets written for Christians on the subject of money adopt an idealist stance, and simply state that your expenditure should not exceed your income, and that you should never borrow. (The extent to which Christians should use credit, and whether they should borrow money at all, is examined later.)

The main purpose of this section, however, is to provide factual information about credit and debt, and to offer some possible solutions to readers who have already discovered for themselves the dangers of getting into debt. It may even be that one of the main reasons you picked up this book was to get some help with your own debt problems.

Cards

Generally speaking, there are three types of 'plastic' widely available: the debit card, the budget card, and the credit card.

Debit cards

Debit cards fall into two categories. One is a charge card, such as American Express. This does not provide credit in the usual sense of the word, although it is true to say that there is a small interval between buying the goods and handing over the money for them. You pay for the goods or services with your card, and you receive a monthly statement showing what you have spent. You are then expected to pay that amount by the due date; you are not allowed to spread your payments or leave anything outstanding on the settlement date.

So although you have not had to pay cash at the shops, this is not a method of obtaining long-term credit. All you achieve is the convenience of not having to carry cash, and you

" . . . the convenience of not having to carry cash . . ."

do receive a few days' credit between the date of purchase and the monthly settlement date.

Another type of debit card is known in the UK as Switch or Delta. Again, you pay for the goods as you would with any card, but the amount charged is debited direct to your bank account, just as if you had written a cheque. As an interesting aside, although the banks' technology would enable your account to be debited on the day of purchase, they delay the debit so that it does not arrive until a day or so later. This is so that card users are not at a disadvantage when compared to shoppers who have written out a cheque. Because a cheque does not clear until at least two days following banking, it was felt that an immediate debit under Switch or Delta would make it difficult for this new concept to become accepted by the public.

It suits the banks to encourage the use of debit cards, however, as they are much more efficient than cheques, and less expensive for the banks to process. It is generally assumed that the writing of cheques at retail outlets will be phased out in due course in favour of debit cards. It will then be interesting to see if the banks start to debit accounts on the day of the transaction, rather than retaining the delay which currently exists.

Verdict: It is unlikely that the use of debit cards would cause debt to mount up, because you have to pay the amounts charged in full. Of course, users of charge cards do have to ensure they don't use them so enthusiastically that they lack the funds to settle. The main advantage of charge cards is the convenience over carrying cash. If you have no objection to carrying cash or using cheques, or doubt your

" . . . you have to pay the amounts charged in full . . ."

self-restraint, then you might as well leave charge cards alone and stick to cash and cheques.

Budget cards
Although budget accounts are offered by banks, this type of arrangement is more frequently available through some of the larger chains of stores.

With a budget account, you arrange to pay a regular amount to the store or bank each month, and this allows you credit up to so many times the monthly payment. For example, you may decide to pay £10 per month, and the shop may grant you 'purchasing power' of, say, twelve times this amount, which would allow you to spend or borrow up to £120.

Verdict: The amount of credit available is limited, and you are not allowed to borrow more than the set amount. Your monthly repayments under this scheme are always the same, and the scope for getting into financial difficulty is rather small. So, in fact, a budget account can prove to be quite a help – although do remember that interest is always payable on the amount you borrow, and the rate payable on budget accounts can be very high. Nothing comes free!

"Nothing comes free!"

Credit cards
With a credit card you are allowed to spend as much as you like, and as often as you like, up to the pre-set credit limit. This credit limit will normally be much higher than it would be under a budget scheme, although it is normally the credit-card company which notifies the amount of credit available to you; you

don't often have a choice. Typically, credit limits will range from £400 to £3,000, depending on your 'credit-worthiness'.

To decide the amount of credit available to you, the credit-card issuer examines your application form, and makes a judgment based on the following factors:

- your occupation
- whether you are employed or self-employed
- your level of income
- whether you are married – and whether your partner works
- whether you own your own home, or are a tenant
- how long you have been at your current address

They take other factors into account too, but these things all go to build up a picture of your ability to cope with the repayments.

Many people use credit cards because, up to a point, they provide free credit. This is because, if you repay everything on your statement by the settlement date shown, you pay no interest. This can mean you have had credit for up to about six weeks free of charge.

"But this is where temptation comes in"

But this is where temptation comes in. Each month you have to pay back at least 5% of the current balance. If you pay only this minimum each month, and continue making enthusiastic use of the card, you will soon reach your credit limit. And once you decide to settle just part of the outstanding balance, you start to pay interest at an incredibly high rate – usually not much less than 20%, and sometimes much more. What started out as an arrangement to tide you over for a few weeks soon turns into a long-term, expensive commitment.

This is where you can so easily get out of your depth.

Verdict: If you are sufficiently disciplined and extremely well organized, you can use credit cards to good effect by making full use of the free credit period. Furthermore, credit cards are widely accepted worldwide, and can be more convenient, and safer, than carrying cash.

You can also use credit cards for telephone shopping, such as buying from a newspaper advertisement, or theatre tickets. This can be extremely convenient.

But the dangers are clear to see. If you allow the debit balance to creep up to, say, £1,000, this will cost you something in the order of £200 a year in interest. This is expensive credit.

"This is expensive credit"

If you feel the need to borrow, you would be much better off arranging a loan through your bank. It will be much cheaper.

*h*ire purchase

Hire purchase is normally available when you buy a major item such as a car or a cooker.

The main difference between hire purchase and any other form of borrowing is that the item you are buying does not actually belong to you until you have completed all the payments, usually over a period of between two and five years. Should you fail to keep up the payments, the goods can be repossessed by the hire-purchase company – and this they certainly will do.

"Hire purchase can end up causing all sorts of headaches"

Again, hire purchase can be an expensive option. It is usually widely available, and many people go for this option because it seems so convenient. If you are buying a car, for instance, it will seem much easier to complete a hire-purchase agreement on the spot, rather than having to face an interview with the bank manager to apply for a loan.

Verdict: Hire purchase can be easy and convenient to arrange, especially for a major purchase such as a car. But you have virtually no security if you fall behind in your payments, and if the car is repossessed it can be difficult to obtain any benefit from the payments made so far. So hire purchase can end up causing all sorts of headaches.

It would be cheaper and more sensible to have a chat with your bank manager to see what he or she would suggest instead.

If you are making a major purchase, there may be a special offer of interest-free credit. This may well be worth looking into, but do bear in mind that the real cost of credit has to be paid in one way or another. It may be that the dealer is, in effect, cutting his profit margin by subsidizing your credit agreement. If this is the case, you may be better off borrowing the money from the bank at a reasonably low rate of interest, and then negotiating a discount for cash from the purchase price.

Having said that, it is sometimes possible to obtain a good deal by taking interest-free credit. For example, you may be able to buy items such as carpets or furniture under an interest-free credit scheme. In cases such as this, it is unlikely you would be able to negotiate a discount from the price if you had the cash – as you can when buying a car – so there is nothing to lose by taking up the credit.

Catalogues

If you buy goods through a catalogue, you will probably have the option of paying on a monthly basis as an alternative to paying in one go. Although this may be convenient, the penalty for paying monthly will be high. Furthermore, monthly schemes like these can encourage the buyer to get carried away, and can be another way of accumulating financial problems.

Bank loans and overdrafts

If you have to borrow money, a visit to your bank should be the first step. The more expensive and risky sources of finance play on the fact that most of us fight shy of a visit to the bank, and they know full well that we would rather hide behind the anonymity of the credit card or hire-purchase company.

This is one reason why bank cash dispensers are proving to be so popular. They were devised to provide customers with a way of obtaining cash outside banking hours. This facility is very convenient. But the banks should ask themselves this question: why is it that their customers would rather queue up in the rain at a cash machine during bank business hours, when they could enter the warm, dry branch and deal with the staff behind the counter? The banks have an image problem.

"Most of us fight shy of a visit to the bank . . ."

Sorting out their image is the banks' job: obtaining a loan on the best terms possible is yours. So it is up to you to pluck up courage to telephone the bank and request an appointment with the manager. He or she will be only too happy to meet you, and to have an opportunity to explain how helpful the bank can be.

But you do need to be reasonably well organized. Banks do not lend money unless they are satisfied that you can afford the repayments. You should take with you a domestic budget, as outlined in chapter 2, and should adapt the budget to take into account your estimate of how much the loan is going to cost each month. If you look well organized, that will be a useful start.

"If you look well organized, that will be a useful start"

A bank loan will be taken out over a set period. For instance, you may wish to borrow £5,000 towards a new car. This would normally be arranged over a period of two or three years.

The longer the period of the loan, the lower your monthly payments are, because you have longer to repay the capital borrowed. Spreading the loan over a long period does mean, however, that the total amount of interest paid is that much higher. So if you don't like the idea of paying too much interest, go for as short a period as you can afford.

An overdraft is simply a current-account facility which allows you to spend more than you actually hold in your account. It is important that an overdraft is approved by the bank before you start over-spending, otherwise you may find the bank will start 'bouncing' your cheques (that is, refusing them for payment).

Verdict: A bank loan will certainly work out cheaper than using a credit card, and a discussion with your bank manager will help you to plan your finances. Although an overdraft can be a helpful arrangement, it will work out more expensive than a bank loan – especially if you go overdrawn without the manager's approval.

If the bank refuses your application for a loan or overdraft, the chances are you shouldn't be borrowing the money anyway.

" . . . cheaper than using a credit card . . ."

Secured or unsecured?

Wherever you borrow money, you should understand the difference between secured and unsecured lending.

A secured loan is when you offer some 'security' to cover the amount of the loan. For example:

- £5,000 borrowed from a finance company to buy a car. The car itself is offered as security, so that if you are unable to keep up the payments, the car can be repossessed.
- £30,000 borrowed in the form of a mortgage on a house. This is another form of secured lending, because if you cannot keep up the payments, the bank or building society can force you to sell the house, and the amount originally borrowed would have to be paid back out of the sale proceeds.
- £1,000 borrowed for a holiday, with your home offered as security. Again, the home

could be put at risk if you cannot meet your obligations under the loan agreement.

An unsecured loan is one where no security is offered. This restricts the amount of 'damage' the bank can do to you if you are unable to keep up with payments.

For example, few banks would make a car loan a secured loan; it would normally be unsecured. This means they have no right to repossess your car if you fall behind with your payments. They would still have the right to take you to court to recover the amounts owed, but an unsecured loan makes it more difficult for the lender to recover money from you in the case of difficulty.

In general, it is safer to have an unsecured loan, although the rate of interest payable is usually slightly higher than it would be for a secured loan.

"There is always someone, somewhere, willing to lend money."

Loan sharks

There is always someone, somewhere, willing to lend money. Some people are so desperate to borrow that they would borrow from anyone. They are the natural victims of loan sharks. Typically, these lenders operate in poorer neighbourhoods and visit their 'customers' from door to door, offering modest amounts, say to buy food, or children's toys at Christmas.

These arrangements are illegal, and no attempt is made to explain to those borrowing just how much the repayments are going to cost. In fact, the real rate of interest charged can be over 200%, and it is hardly surprising that such arrangements end in misery.

If you are ever tempted to borrow under this kind of informal arrangement, *don't do it*.

Credit unions

A credit union is established as a local initiative, perhaps catering just for a particular housing estate. Those who have some money to invest may deposit their money with the union in exchange for a modest rate of interest. Others may borrow from the union, also at a modest rate of interest, and the whole principle operates on a self-help basis. The union is set up and run by local people, and there are no shareholders to take a profit; it exists only for the benefit of its members.

Information about setting one up may be obtained by writing to the Association of British Credit Unions (see 'Where to get help' at the end of the book).

The pressure to borrow

I've explained how to borrow money, but please don't take this as encouragement to borrow. It's up to you to decide for yourself whether or not it is right for you to borrow in certain situations, but you do need to be aware of the commercial pressures around us.

We have to determine for ourselves the difference between necessities and luxuries. So next time you are about to borrow money, either in a formal way, or by using a credit card, ask yourself the following questions:

" . . . the difference between necessities and luxuries . . ."

- Do I need what I am about to buy? Am I being persuaded by advertising that what I have seen is a necessity when it is nothing of the kind?
- What is my motive for the purchase? Again, is it a need, or something to impress others?
- Would it be better if I delayed the expenditure until I could afford it?
- How far does my overall level of spending detract from my ability to give to the Lord's work?

In the next chapter we examine the plight of Billy and Sandra, whose finances have run out of control – mainly because they have borrowed much too enthusiastically.

CREDIT AND DEBT

Billy and Sandra's story

This is the story of Billy and Sandra Cooper. They have been married for six years and have two young daughters.

Billy and Sandra both work. Billy is a psychiatric nurse, and Sandra works at the same hospital as a staff nurse.

Sandra always felt it was Billy's job to look after the finances, so she left him to monitor their joint bank account and pay the bills at the right time. Sandra would rather not look at the bank statement each month; she left all that to Billy, but would always check with him before spending over £30 or so. But because they usually went shopping together, it was not often that either would spend anything without the other's knowing.

"Sandra would rather not look at the bank statement each month . . ."

"... surprised that, once again, they were right up to the agreed overdraft limit"

Most families find it a struggle to keep afloat financially, but the Coopers were finding it increasingly difficult to manage. They were now using four different plastic cards fairly frequently, and had a number of other regular commitments which were swallowing up a substantial amount of their joint monthly income; as well as the usual mortgage and fuel bills, and so on, they were repaying three loans totalling £260 a month.

Each month Billy would add up the amounts due for the various bills and credit companies, taking into account the regular payments under standing orders. He would then examine the bank statement and would be surprised that, once again, they were right up to the agreed overdraft limit. Billy would then calculate the effect on the bank balance of the two salaries being paid in, and this would tell him how much he could afford to pay off on the credit cards.

Billy and Sandra had not originally intended to use their credit cards all that much. But they were attracted by the idea of using the free-credit period between the date of spending and the settlement date, on which they would repay the amount owing in full. That was the original intention. It's very tempting to settle just part of the amount outstanding, though, with the intention of settling the balance during the following month. But it doesn't work out in reality if you use the card in the meantime, as this only increases the amount due the following month.

This is exactly what happened in the case of the Coopers. Billy was finding it more difficult to repay the amounts owing on the cards, and he started paying off just the minimum amount each month – while still using the cards in the meantime.

Eventually the inevitable happened. Billy found it was impossible to pay all the monthly commitments and the minimum amounts due on the credit cards and stay within the agreed overdraft limit with the bank.

The first month this happened, Billy decided he would still make the payments, and hoped for the best. Naturally, the result was a request from the bank to stay within the 'agreed facility', and a reminder that the need to generate such letters entitles the bank to debit the account with a £15 charge – which just made matters worse.

The following month, Billy decided he couldn't face being in trouble with the bank again, and so he omitted payment to one of the credit cards, with the intention of paying them double next month. This didn't cause too much trouble, except that his next card statement contained a strict reminder to keep up to date with payments.

The situation was no better in the third month, but no problem. Billy managed to pay the increased amount due under the credit card which was now in arrears, at the expense of one of the other cards. But Billy should have seen a bigger problem coming; carrying on like this would simply bring things grinding to a halt. He didn't have to wait that long.

'Billy! I had a terrible experience today. I was so embarrassed.' Sandra was sitting at the kitchen table and hadn't attempted to make the evening meal. She burst into tears as soon as Billy came in through the door.

'What is it, love?'

'Well, you know I told you this morning I

"Eventually the inevitable happened"

was working a half day, so I would do the shopping, and I asked you how I should pay this week, and you told me to use the Visa card? I spent half an hour going round that rotten supermarket, and when I got to the checkout, and packaged everything up, they wouldn't accept my card. I didn't take my cheque-book because you told me to use the card, so I had no other way to pay. I was furious. I told the girl at the checkout to get the supervisor. After all, we've been going there for years. They know us. Surely there was some mistake.

'But the supervisor said there was nothing she could do. All she knew was that my card had been rejected.'

'So what did you do?' Billy asked.

"I just stood there looking stupid"

'There was nothing I could do. I just stood there looking stupid. I had to leave my loaded-up trolley behind. In fact, I ran out of the supermarket as quickly as I could. I suppose they had to unpack the trolley and put all our food back. Are you going to phone Visa to sort them out? How can they do this to us? I'll never be able to face going back to that shop ever again.'

Billy knew full well why the problem had occurred. The accumulated arrears under the Visa card meant they were now over the credit limit, and so Visa had put a stop on future transactions.

That evening Billy and Sandra had a long talk. Billy didn't hold back any longer. He brought Sandra up to date. She could not believe how far things had got out of control.

Sandra criticized Billy because he hadn't kept things under control.

Billy criticized Sandra because she never

expressed any interest in how the bills were paid, and he accused her of being extravagant.

The Coopers were in danger of splitting up. They were so busy accusing each other of being at fault that they did not realize the effect this was having on their relationship. The crunch came one morning when a letter came from Visa. This was an official notice under the Consumer Credit Act concerning the arrears. The letter contained a warning that proceedings would commence unless the arrears were paid off immediately.

And that wasn't all. The same post brought a similar letter from the car-loan company. Billy had let the payments fall into arrears, and the company was threatening to come and repossess the car unless further payments were made. This was the last straw.

Before we see what happened next, let's have a detailed look at the Coopers' monthly outgoings.

". . . an official notice under the Consumer Credit Act . . ."

	Amount outstanding	Minimum monthly payment
Mortgage	65,000	480.00
Gas		35.00
Electricity		30.00
Telephone		35.00
Insurance		50.00
Council tax		80.00
Water rates		25.00
Car loan	3,500	85.00
Credit card: Mastercard	1,900	95.00
Credit card: Visa	2,300	115.00
Store card: budget account	185	10.00
Store card: credit account	750	40.00

Loan for kitchen equipment	3,100	100.00
Loan for lounge furniture	2,800	75.00

The capital amount outstanding came to £14,535, excluding the mortgage.

The total monthly payments came to £1,255 per month, and this did not allow anything for ordinary expenditure such as petrol and entertainment, or for necessaries such as food and clothing.

The Coopers should have been in a reasonably good position, because Billy and Sandra were both working, and brought home a total income of £1,300 a month after all deductions for tax, National Insurance and pensions. It is not difficult to see that, after deducting their regular commitments, this left only £45 a month for food and other necessaries. Even with their child benefit, this was not enough for a family of four.

" . . . not enough for a family of four . . ."

Understandably enough, the Coopers continued to spend much more than £45 per month, which explains why it had become impossible to pay all the commitments in full each month.

So what were the Coopers' options from here?

Billy still assumed the main responsibility to get things right, but he did not really know what to do. A number of options occurred to him.

1. Perhaps he could omit the payment for the mortgage for just a month or two. This would allow him to catch up on some of his arrears and provide the family with some spending-money for a while. After all, he was having to pay the building society £480 a

month, so if he could be relieved of having to pay this for just a short time, it would be a real help.

2. As an alternative, Billy had noticed a number of advertisements for loans in his local paper. He wondered whether it would be possible to take out a new loan to repay all his credit-card borrowings. At least this would get the credit-card companies off his back, and the new loan may work out cheaper.

3. Billy wondered whether it would be possible to negotiate an increased overdraft with the bank, but he soon dismissed this idea. He hated having to meet the bank manager, and anyway he had received a number of unpleasant letters from the bank recently, so he could hardly expect them to increase the overdraft facility.

4. Perhaps there was an organization he could go to where he could get some help. This last option didn't appeal to Billy at all, because deep down he knew he had been extremely foolish, and he didn't want to be forced into a situation where he would have to disclose the full horror of the family's financial state.

Billy decided to go for the second option, so he telephoned one of the loan companies which had advertised in the paper. They asked him a few questions to establish whether the Coopers would qualify. The loan company soon lost interest when they learnt that the outstanding mortgage of £65,000 represented over 85% of the estimated present value of the house. Furthermore, they doubted whether the Coopers would be able to afford the repayments, even though the rate of interest would indeed be considerably

" . . . the full horror of the family's financial state . . . "

"He was sure he could get away without having to pay . . ."

lower than the credit-card companies were charging.

Billy knew they had a point.

It was again that time of the month when more payments had to be made. Billy now plumped for option 1. He was sure he could get away without having to pay the building society, at least for one month. This relieved the tension perfectly, because all the credit-card payments were made, together with the gas, electricity and other regular bills, and there was still sufficient left to buy the food. Billy was pleasantly surprised when the end of the month arrived, and there was no letter from the building society.

Just as Billy was considering his options for the fifth month, however, the inevitable letter from the building society did arrive, so Billy knew this was the end of that option. Something else had to be done.

Billy's brother, John, worked for an insurance company, and Billy decided to have a chat with him on the phone to see if he had any bright ideas.

John listened patiently to Billy's sorry tale, and Billy was relieved when John didn't take the expected judgmental approach. John said there was only one thing to do: get proper help, which meant going for debt counselling. *Debt counselling!* How could he possibly go for that? The very thought of this was enough to make Billy consider leaving home and putting his problems behind him. He quickly brought his telephone conversation with his brother to an end and hung up.

But when he had calmed down, Billy realized that everything was now totally out of control, and that he really would have to get some help. Now was the time to swallow his pride, admit his mistakes and try to get things right.

He telephoned John again, and apologized for his attitude. Where could he go for debt counselling?

*d*ebt counselling

John told him that debt counselling is not as scary as it sounds. 'But it does involve a thorough investigation of everything to do with your finances, and it'll help you understand your own situation better,' he explained. 'The best place to start is the Citizens Advice Bureau.' John knew from his own dealings in financial matters that the extent of help available with debt matters varied enormously from region to region.

So the Coopers went along to the local Citizens Advice Bureau, who put them in touch with a debt counsellor. This is what she was able to do for them.

She arranged a meeting with the Coopers, and insisted that both Billy and Sandra were present. She explained that it was important to ensure that both husband and wife were aware of the whole picture.

The counsellor helped Billy and Sandra draw up a domestic budget along the lines of the table in chapter 2. She encouraged the Coopers to insert realistic amounts for food and clothing, and also made sure that the budget included everything.

She then identified those items on the list which were absolutely essential for payment each month, and highlighted those debts

"Now was the time to swallow his pride"

"Debt counselling is not as scary as it sounds"

"The most important was the mortgage payment"

which could cause them the most harm if they were not kept up to date. Of course, the most important was the mortgage payment, and the officer was horrified to learn that Billy had missed a payment without even discussing this with the building society.

It became clear that there were a number of regular payments which were not exactly essential from the family's point of view and which, if not paid promptly, would cause only a limited problem. In the main, these were the payments to the credit cards, the store cards and the loans for the kitchen equipment and furniture. The counsellor was not advocating ignoring these commitments, but was simply pointing out that they would have to be the lowest priority, in view of the fact that the extent to which the companies could cause problems was limited.

For instance, Billy and Sandra had been under the impression that anything they had purchased using a credit card could be repossessed by the card company in the event that payments were not kept up to date, but the counsellor was able to explain that this was not the case. They had no right to come and repossess anything.

The next step was to remove from the list of payments the amounts to the credit-card and loan companies. Deducting the remaining payments from the Coopers' joint monthly income showed how much money was available to share between the loan companies.

They then listed these debts, showing the amounts outstanding and the minimum payments due in accordance with the credit agreements. This showed that although the loan companies were due to receive a total of £435 a month, the domestic budget showed that the Coopers could afford to pay only £220 a month.

This was the part that impressed Billy and Sandra. The officer calculated how much of the available £220 should be paid to each credit company. She did this by working out some figures in proportion to the amount owed. The revised payment schedule then looked like this:

"This was the part that impressed Billy and Sandra"

	Amount outstanding	Minimum monthly payment	Proposed monthly payment
Credit card: Mastercard	1,900	95.00	37.88
Credit card: Visa	2,300	115.00	45.86
Store card: budget account	185	10.00	3.68
Store card: credit account	750	40.00	14.95
Loan for kitchen equipment	3,100	100.00	61.80
Loan for lounge furniture	2,800	75.00	55.83
Total monthly payment		435.00	220.00

The counsellor then drafted a letter for Billy and Sandra to send to each of the loan companies. The letter explained that the Coopers were in financial difficulty, and enclosed a copy of the domestic budget. The letter went on to offer the loan company the reduced payment as calculated above.

Billy and Sandra were staggered to learn that, with a little persuasion, the companies would accept the reduced payments, at least for the time being. The Coopers were told that

". . . asked the loan companies to stop adding interest . . ."

the companies would want to keep in regular contact with them, and would push for an increase in payments, especially if there was an increase in income at some stage.

Billy and Sandra were particularly impressed by one paragraph in the letter which asked the loan companies to stop adding interest to the outstanding amount. They could hardly believe that the companies would do this.

The counsellor looked at Billy and Sandra's wide-open mouths, and explained why the loan companies would accept the reduced amounts. Although the companies had the right to take legal proceedings against them for non-payment, they knew full well that all the court would do would be to find a level at which the family could afford to repay. What was being offered would forestall a court action. The loan companies would see for themselves that they would be no better off if they decided to take the Coopers to court.

facing the problem

It is all too easy to say that there is no sense in allowing debt to get out of hand, or even that it is better not to borrow money at all. The fact is, people do allow huge debts to mount up, and that includes plenty of Christians.

One of the main things to get hold of, therefore, is what to do if you find that things have got out of control.

This is no small point. Suicides often occur because of financial problems and, again, Christians are not immune to this sort of pressure. Suicide arises from despair. Yet perfectly acceptable solutions to financial problems can normally be found if the people involved can find the strength to admit their problems and then obtain some proper advice.

So admit the problem. Face it. Talk about it. If you are married, make sure your husband or wife knows the full extent of the problem. Pray about the problem. Visit the Citizens Advice Bureau. Take action based on their advice. Don't assume you can handle the problem on your own, as that will only lead to despair.

The Christian organization Credit Action can provide valuable help. You can contact them on the freephone number shown in the 'Where to get help' section at the end of this book.

"Don't assume you can handle the problem on your own"

THE AGONY COLUMN

Have a go at working out your own answers before you read mine.

Q Is it right for a Christian to borrow money? How can the purchase of goods with money we haven't got be honouring to God?

A Problems with finances are not new. When Nehemiah set about the task of rebuilding the walls of Jerusalem, one problem which came to light was the profiteering of some of the rich at the expense of those who were so poor that they were having to borrow for life's necessaries. 'You are exacting usury

"Is it right for a Christian to borrow money?"

MANAGING YOUR MONEY

(Nehemiah 5:7)

from your own countrymen!' Nehemiah accused the rich noblemen. He went on to say that some of those engaged in the rebuilding were lending money to each other without interest, and so why couldn't the rich lenders do the same?

The Bible does seem to place most of the responsibility to behave reasonably on to the shoulders of those who are doing the lending, rather than the borrowing. What upset Nehemiah more than anything was that the Jews who were charging interest were doing so in a situation where the money was being borrowed for necessaries rather than luxuries.

Perhaps there is something we can learn from the distinction between what is absolutely necessary, and what is a luxury. It can prove to be extremely difficult to draw this distinction in a modern, materialistic society, but nevertheless it may help us decide whether or not it is right for us to borrow.

If you reach the conclusion that you are not going to borrow under any circumstances, it may be rather difficult to put this resolve into practice. Most people will want to own their own home, but, for the majority, this would not be possible without taking out a mortgage. If it is right to borrow money to buy a house, can it be wrong to borrow for our other needs?

The money that Billy and Sandra had borrowed over the years had, in the main, been for luxuries. Doubtless it would have been wiser if they had waited until they had saved some money before committing themselves to such expense. It is too easy to borrow without appreciating just how much the interest is costing us – and that is money which can often be put to better use.

" . . . without appreciating just how much the interest is costing us . . ."

CREDIT AND DEBT

Q **My friend is having financial problems, and I would like to lend him some of the money I have saved in the building society. We have both agreed that I should charge the same rate of interest I currently receive on this account – so I shall be no worse off, and it will be much cheaper for my friend than borrowing from the bank. Is there any reason why I shouldn't do this?**

A *Please be very careful. Many friendships have been broken because such an arrangement has gone wrong. Your friend will be very grateful that you are able to lend him the money, but it will be a different matter if it turns out he is unable to repay you.*

If it really is that important that your friend should have this money, perhaps you should consider making it an interest-free loan. This will be even more appreciated, and the lack of interest will make repayment easier.

Better still, consider making a gift. This way, there is no danger to your friendship should your friend's circumstances deteriorate.

If you do lend money, you should not lend more than you are prepared to lose. Keeping the friendship will prove more valuable than the money.

Going back to the principle of what Nehemiah said: if we are in a position to use our money to help others, we should think carefully before charging interest. Otherwise, we may not be helping at all.

PAYING TAXES AND PLANNING FOR THE FUTURE

9

*W*hy do Christians have to pay tax?

'In this world nothing can be said to be certain, except death and taxes.' So said Benjamin Franklin. Although, as a Christian, you may look forward to everlasting life, there is no escape from taxes.

Indeed, if there were any doubt about it, the words of our Lord would dispel it. In saying, 'Give to Caesar what is Caesar's, and to God what is God's,' he makes it quite clear that the Christian has a fiscal responsibility to the secular government as well as a spiritual responsibility.

(Matthew 22:21)

Nonetheless, this simple statement, as well as our Lord's teaching to the tax-collectors of his time, deals with a number of problems that Christians invent for themselves today.

'My Christian commitment prevents my contributing to the manufacture of nuclear bombs. In fact, I am a pacifist and will not pay towards the upkeep of the armed services.' Thus some people argue when refusing to pay the tax assessed on them. Some go to the extent of working out the defence budget as a percentage of total government expenditure, and try to withhold the same percentage of their tax bill.

They are entitled to their views, and this is not the place to debate the peacekeeping role of the armed services today. I do not believe, however, that these views truly reflect Christ's teaching. Just think of the context in which the Lord spoke. The Jews were under the rule of Rome as well as their own rulers. The whole area was occupied by a Roman force, the people being kept in line by an occupying army of Roman soldiers.

In this context, then, the Lord told those who listened that Caesar was entitled to what was his. The head of the occupying country was entitled to collect taxes, those same taxes that would pay the soldiers who were busy extending the Roman Empire and oppressing the conquered peoples. Caesar was entitled to the taxes because he was the ruler. What he did with the money was a matter for his own conscience.

Again, Caesar was entitled only to what was rightfully his. The Lord taught that the tax-collectors had to pay back (with compensation) money taken from individuals

"Caesar was entitled to the taxes . . ."

in excess of their true liability. There is no virtue in paying more tax than is required of you.

*h*ow much tax should a Christian pay?

Today, taxes on income and profits are assessed by Her Majesty's Inspectors of Taxes and collected by Collectors of Taxes. Together they are known as the Inland Revenue. Their power is granted under the annual Finance Acts produced after each Budget and by case law from the courts. The right of an individual to pay the minimum amount of tax he is required to pay is enshrined in a number of legal cases. Lord Clyde, the Lord President of the Court of Session, expressed this right in these words:

No man in this country is under the smallest obligation, moral or other, so to arrange his legal relations to his business or to his property as to enable the Inland Revenue to put the largest possible shovel into his stores. The Inland Revenue is not slow – and quite rightly – to take every advantage which is open to it under the taxing statutes for the purpose of depleting the taxpayer's pocket. And the taxpayer is, in like manner, entitled to be astute to prevent, so far as he honestly can, the depletion of his means by the Inland Revenue.

Christians should have no conscience about arranging their affairs legally to avoid the effects of taxation. Indeed, the use of covenants and Gift Aid as described in chapter 4 is exactly such an arrangement. Making gifts out of taxed income when the recipient could

". . . arranging their affairs legally to avoid the effects of taxation . . ."

benefit from a repayment of tax as well as from the gift is a clear example of poor stewardship.

It is good stewardship to pay the minimum tax.

Whereas tax *avoidance* along the lines described should be perfectly acceptable to the Christian, tax *evasion* is an entirely different matter. Tax evasion implies the use of fraud or concealment to escape the effects of taxation. I am sure you are thinking that you would do nothing illegal. That may be so, although I shall look at a common problem in a moment. The very state of doing nothing can also be illegal.

Ignorance and carelessness can lead to tax evasion. It is every taxpayer's responsibility to notify the Inland Revenue as soon as they put themselves in a position to receive taxable income. If you regularly receive an annual tax return, it's usually sufficient to enter sources of income that have started in the previous tax year. If the tax office has never sent you a return form, that does not relieve you of your responsibility to notify it of your income.

Remember, too, that *all* income has to be declared. This is so whether or not income tax has been deducted from the money before you receive it.

In 1990 the law changed, and a wife is now required to inform the Inland Revenue of her own income and claim her allowances, rather than relying on her husband to do it for her.

I wonder whether you have ever sent a gift to a Christian organization or to your church, and the treasurer has asked you to consider making the gift under a deed of covenant. The benefits of the covenant to the organization

"The very state of doing nothing can be illegal"

117

*"Even
Parliament
realized that
this was all a
little silly . . ."*

have been explained and you have gladly signed the form. Perhaps you didn't date your signature, or maybe you were asked to date the form with the same date as your cheque.

Backdating a deed of covenant, however, is illegal and is technically tax evasion. By the way, if the organization had refrained from banking your cheque until after you had signed the deed, or asked you for another cheque or even to re-date the original payment, then you (and they) would not have broken the law. Even Parliament realized that this was all a little silly, and when Gift Aid was introduced it was made quite clear that the form could be signed after the cheque had been sent and banked.

*t*axes on income and gains

Most paid workers are employees, and our tax and National Insurance contributions are collected from us payday by payday under the Pay As You Earn (PAYE) system. There is little that can go wrong and, on the whole, the correct amount of tax will be paid. Do check the figures from time to time, however, and, if there is something you do not understand, ask the Inspector to explain it. His or her name and address will be on any communication (such as a Coding Notice) which has been sent to you, and is also available from your employer.

If you are self-employed, the method of collecting tax from you is more complicated, especially in the opening years of a new business and in the closing years of an old one. There are also moves afoot to change the whole tax system for the self-employed. My advice would be for you to contact an accountant who will be able to explain matters to you and give you advice on legally reducing your tax bill. (Remember, tax avoidance is quite legal and does not contradict a Christian testimony.)

Whether employed or self-employed, if you make any profits from the sale of things you own, then this profit may be assessed for capital gains tax. There are some exemptions; profits from the sale of your own home or your car are examples. Capital gains tax can be charged even if you give the items away. The safest way would be to discuss the situation with an accountant, who will be able to help you.

*t*axes on spending

So far we have looked at *direct* taxes – taxes on income or capital gains we receive. There are also taxes on what we spend. The most common of these indirect taxes is Value Added Tax (VAT). This tax is administered not by the Inland Revenue, but by Her Majesty's Customs and Excise, and another complex set of rules is attached to it. Problems with VAT can arise for the Christian in business, but as long as the basic rule that evasion is wrong is followed, then a proper Christian witness can be maintained.

*t*axes on giving and taxes on dying

Inheritance tax is chargeable on the value of what you own when you die. It can also be payable if you give away money or articles during your lifetime. (There are exemptions, and these are explained below.) Now you are probably thinking that this doesn't apply to you because you don't have any money! But if you have a company pension scheme that pays death-in-service benefits, or a mortgage endowment or protection policy, or any other life assurance policy, you will actually leave an estate that could be quite valuable.

"If you are blessed with wealthy parents . . ."

If you are blessed with wealthy parents, a tactful word with them might reduce a future tax bill. Care must be taken, of course, to avoid emulating the prodigal son, taking your inheritance and frittering it away. That would not be good stewardship.

What, then, are the rules? The same rules apply to lifetime gifts as well as to legacies left in your will. All gifts to registered charities and to places of worship are exempt from any charge to inheritance tax. An annual amount of £3,000 (changed in the annual Budget) can also be given away to other people and organizations, exempt from tax. Gifts by one spouse to the other are exempt.

On other gifts, inheritance tax is charged at two rates. The first rate, 0%, is charged on the first £150,000 (changed each year in the Budget) of the value of your estate. This is known as the nil rate band. The remainder is charged at 40%. Lifetime gifts are usually charged at half this rate. There are complications depending on how soon after making the gift the donor dies, or whether the gift was to an individual or to a trust. Tax law is not simple, and the law relating to inheritance tax is no exception. If after reading this you feel you have a problem, or simply have further questions, you must consult a good tax accountant or tax lawyer.

Making a will

Even if you say that all this talk of inheritance tax isn't relevant to you, you should make a will. A will is simply a document that indicates to those who survive you how they should deal with your affairs. In your will you can dispose of your property, but you can also indicate your preference for burial or cremation, the type of service you would prefer, and even the hymns you would like sung.

If none of this interests you because you will be in a far better place by then, do consider those who are left behind. Many people believe that if they make no will, all their property will go to their husband or wife anyway. This is not the case. In fact, your spouse would receive all your property to do with as he or she wished, only if, when you died:

- you left no living children or descendants of your children ('children' includes illegitimate or adopted children, but not stepchildren);
- you had no parents living;
- you left no brothers or sisters or their children.

" . . . because you will be in a far better place by then . . ."

In all other cases various of these relatives would receive some of your estate, and your spouse would be entitled only to the income arising on part of your estate.

Apart from anything else, this is messy and expensive in terms of legal fees. It is easy to make a will; there are many readable books on the subject to help you write your own simple will, or you can ask a solicitor to draw one up for you.

Wills can be added to (by codicil) or changed (by writing a new one) as many times as you like. If you have made a will and your family would like to divide up your estate in a way different from what you suggested, then they may do so providing all the beneficiaries agree. If you have not made a will, then the law states how your property is to be divided, and it cannot be changed.

" . . . it is invalid as soon as you marry . . ."

If you draw up a will before you marry, then it is invalid as soon as you marry. This is so unless you clearly state within the will that it was written in contemplation of your marriage to a specific, named, person and that it was not your intention that the will (or specific clauses in it) should be revoked on marriage.

You may have anyone to look after your affairs after you die until your estate is distributed. These people are known as your executors or trustees and must be over eighteen years of age. Beneficiaries under a will cannot be witnesses to your signature. Executors can be witnesses, or they can be beneficiaries, but they cannot be both.

Without being silly about it, do think of contingencies. You may wish to leave everything to your wife, but if she dies in an accident with you, what happens then? Include some alternative plans unless you want the will to follow the rules of intestacy. It is good practice, by the way, when leaving large portions of your estate to individuals, to state that they are entitled to the property only if they are still alive thirty days after your death. Apart from avoiding complications of deciding who died first in the case of an accidental death involving you and your beneficiary, it avoids a double charge to inheritance tax in the same situation.

THE AGONY COLUMN

Have a go at working out your own answers before you read mine.

Q I want someone to look after my garden and do odd repair jobs about the house. Someone I know has fallen on hard times and in a spirit of Christian love I have asked him for an estimate of the cost and he has quoted me a price. He insists, however, that I must pay in cash, not by cheque. He tells me that this will save me money. I do not understand this at all.

A If you stop and think you will realize the implication of his statement. You are being asked to pay cash for a job of work. There will be no written trace of the transaction as far as you are concerned, and certainly no trace as far as the workman is concerned. This would enable him to get away with not

"No-one could prove that the money had changed hands"

declaring the amount he charges you for tax, or VAT. No-one could prove that the money had changed hands. He tells you that the job will be cheaper because not paying these two taxes can mean that he will make the same profit on the job by charging you only two-thirds of what the proper cost would be, should he declare the income.

Not only that; if your friend has fallen on hard times, he may well be receiving Social Security benefits. If this is the case, then any money he earns should be reported to the Benefits Agency, and his benefits may have to be reduced. Of course, if he is paid in cash, who is to know what he has been paid?

As a Christian you should be very wary of such situations. You would be involving yourself in an illegal act. The insistence on a proper invoice and receipt may not be popular, but it is the right course. It also has advantages for you as well, but that is not really the point at issue. Do remember, though, that a business must be making quite a lot of profit before it is required by law to pay VAT. Do not worry if your proper invoice from a one-person or small firm does not include VAT. That can be perfectly legal, and you have carried out your obligation.

"It depends how much money you want to let them have . . ."

Q **I want to give some money to some missionary friends I have. Can I just send them a cheque?**

A You can, but I suspect that this is not the best way. Obviously it depends how much money you want to let them have, and the purpose for which the money is to be used. If you simply wish to have fellowship with them in their work, then a gift to the missionary society is better. You could ask the society to designate the gift to the particular work of your friends. You would be able to use Gift Aid or a covenant, and providing you pay tax, the society would be able to claim the tax back.

You may wish to provide them with funds to help purchase their own home when they retire. You could arrange (with their cooperation) an endowment policy (which grows in value over the years and requires regular premiums) and pay the premiums on the policy for them. Quite a considerable benefit could be achieved by utilizing the annual tax-free gift exemption. Do take proper advice on this first, though.

Q I know of Christ's teachings to the rich young ruler, and of his repeated admonition to sell what you have and give it to the poor. Although I may not give much away while I am alive, I shall make a will leaving everything to charity when I die.

A First, if you are so concerned about the poor, and the sick and the disadvantaged, we have already looked at a number of ways they can be helped in a tax-efficient manner while you are still alive.

Secondly, writing such a will may be fine if you are older and you and your spouse have built up your own savings and have some financial independence. None of us knows, however, when and how the Lord will call us home. I believe we all have responsibilities to our wives or husbands and families. Do not be so concerned with good works that you leave your family destitute.

" . . . so concerned with good works that you leave your family destitute . . ."

WHERE TO GET HELP

General

British Insurance and Investment Brokers Association (BIIBA)
BIIBA House
14 Bevis Marks
London EC3A 7NT
(0171–623 9043).

IFA Promotions (for a list of independent financial advisers in your area)
Fourth Floor, 28 Grenville Street
London EC1N 8SU
(0171–831 4027)

Personal Investment Authority (PIA)
Consumer Help Desk
Hertsmere House
Hertsmere Road
London E14 4AB
(0171–538 8860)

Banking Ombudsman Bureau
Citadel House
5–11 Fetter Lane
London EC4A 1BR
(0171–583 1395).

Insurance Ombudsman Bureau
City Gate One
135 Park Street,
London SE1 9EA
(0171–928 4488).

Dealing with debt

- Halifax Building Society have published a booklet entitled *Dealing With Debt – A Practical Approach*. This is available free of charge from any Halifax branch. Alternatively, write to:
Halifax Building Society
Trinity Road
Halifax
West Yorkshire HX1 2RG

- A Christian book is available entitled *Escape from Debt*. This is published jointly by **Credit Action** and the **Evangelical Alliance**, and is available from:
Evangelical Alliance
Whitefield House
186 Kennington Park Road
London SE11 4BT
The book costs £2.50 including postage (cheques payable to Evangelical Alliance).

- Details on forming a credit union are available from:
Association of British Credit Unions
Unit 307, Westminster Business Square
339 Kennington Lane
London SE11 5QY
(0171–582 2626)
Credit Action Debt Helpline 0800 591084

*C*ovenant gift schemes (See chapter 4)

Impact Giving UK Trust
1221 Rochdale Road
Blackley
Manchester M9 2EG
(0161–795 7255)

Macedonian (Evangelical) Trust
6 Eastmead Close
Bickley
Bromley
Kent BR1 2JG
(0181–467 8339)

Sovereign Giving (formerly North Staffordshire Evangelical Trust)
6 Heatherwood Close
Thorpe End
Norwich
Norfolk NR13 5BN
(01603 700174)

United Kingdom Evangelization Trust
Latchett Hall
Latchett Road
South Woodford
London E18 1DL
(0181–505 5224)